NEW ENGLAND INSTITUTE
OF TECHNOLOGY
LEARNING RESOURCES CENTER

Architectural Press Library of Planning and Design

Housing for Elderly People

HOUSING FOR ELDERLY PEOPLE

A Guide for Architects, Interior Designers and their Clients

by Martin Valins BA(Hons), DipArch, RIBA

**The Architectural Press: London
Van Nostrand Reinhold Company: New York**

First published in 1988 by
The Architectural Press Ltd,
33 Bowling Green Lane,
London EC1R 0DA

ISBN 0-442-20573-2

Printed in Great Britain

Published in the U.S. and Canada by
Van Nostrand Reinhold Company Inc.
115 Fifth Avenue
New York, New York 10003

Distributed in Canada by
Macmillan of Canada
Division of Canada Publishing Corporation
164 Commander Boulevard
Agincourt, Ontario M1S 3C7, Canada

16 15 14 13 12 11 10 9 8 7 6 5 4 3 2 1

This book is dedicated to my dear parents,
Maisie and Hymie Valins, and in memory of my
late grandfather, Benjamin Copen.

Contents

Acknowledgements

Apart from researching the published information in this subject area I felt it important to speak to the practitioners in this field. That is, those who design the buildings as well as those who have experience in working with and caring for elderly people within the range of facilities that will be discussed in this book. I have therefore written the book in such a format that these specialists, who I have listed below, can address the reader directly where they are quoted throughout the text. I am particularly indebted to them for giving up many hours of their time and to offering highly practical and relevant information based upon many years of experience in the field.

John Eatwell DipArch RIBA,
Architect,
Stanford Eatwell & Associates,
England.

Michael Foster AA Dipl MA MSIAD RIBA,
Architect,
The Tooley & Foster Partnership,
England.

Paul Gibson DipArch(Poly) ARIBA,
Architect,
Sidell Gibson Partnership,
England.

Russell L. Greway AIA,
Architect,
Sullivan Associates,
United States of America.

Gisela Hill MBA,
Executive Vice President,
The Pine Run Community,
United States of America.

Sandra C. Howell Phd MPH,
Associate Professor of Behavioral Science,
Massachusetts Institute of Technology,
United States of America.

Joe Jordan FAIA
Architect,
Jordan Mitchell Inc.,
United States of America.

M. Powell Lawton Phd,
Director of Research,
Philadelphia Geriatric Center,
United States of America.

Pauline O'Driscoll SRN RMN,
Nurse with special interest in care of elderly people in the community, England.

Peter Phippen OBE DipArch(RWA) RIBA,
Architect,
Phippen Randall & Parkes,
England.

Anne Roberts MB BS MRCP,
Geriatrician with special interest in the care of elderly people in the community,
England.

Gilbert A. Rosenthal AIA,
Architect,
Wallace Roberts & Todd,
United States of America.

Geoffrey Salmon FRIBA FSIAD AADip(Hons),
Architect,
Salmon Speed Associates,
England.

Richard Stephan,
Executive Director,
Waverly Heights Life Care Community,
United States of America.

Andrew T. Sullivan AIA AICP,
Architect,
Sullivan Associates,
United States of America.

John White,
Residential Care Manager,
Help The Aged,
England.

I would also like to express my sincere thanks and gratitude to the many wardens, house managers and residents I had the privilege to spend time with. Also to the following people and organisations for their invaluable help:

The Architects' & Building Group (Department of Education and Science), Bain Swan, Peter Barefoot & Partners, Gordon Benoy and Partners, Richard Bettesworth (Anchor Housing Association), David Bland (Help the Aged) David Bull (City of Southampton), Susan Carmichael (Brock Carmichael Associates), London Borough of Croydon, John Dennett (Abbeyfield Buckinghamshire Society), Joc Fisher (Anchor Housing Association), Michael Francis, London Borough of Hammersmith, John Holt (City of Southampton), Christine Hunt (The Guiness Trust), Hutchison Lock & Monk, Jenny Huxley (Ruskin Homes), Mayo Larkin (Larkin Glassman & Prager Associates Inc), Kenneth McDonald (Marriott Corporation), Marden & Knight, Milton Keynes Development Corporation, London Borough of Redbridge, ARP Anthony Richardson & Partners, Brian Roberts (Home Life Care), Mathew Robotham Associates, Noel Shuttleworth (The English Courtyard Association), Michael Southcombe (Wimpey Homes Holdings Ltd), Sharon Townsend (BUPA Care for the Elderly), Michael Twigg Brown & Partners, Maritz Vandenberg (The Architectural Press Ltd).

Illustrations by Tom Owen. All photographs, unless otherwise stated, by the author.

Special thanks to Elaine Span and Linda Gerson for their assistance during my research in the United States.

Finally, Linda Valins, who typed the manuscript and without whose untiring help, support, love and encouragement this book would not have been possible.

Introduction

Demand for purpose-built housing for elderly people already exceeds supply. Both the United States and Great Britain, as nations, are becoming older. That is, more of their populations will be reaching old age than ever before.

It has been estimated that by the turn of the century the elderly population in the USA will grow by at least 59%, and represent 18% of the population: that is 55 million people aged 65 and over[1]. The proportion of those aged 85 years and over is expected to triple.

The United Kingdom is reported to have a similar demographic profile. Whilst the actual numbers of those over pensionable age has risen by 10% over the past decade, to just under 10 million (17.7% of the total UK population), the figure is not expected to rise any further. However, the proportion of those aged 75 years and over will increase by 21% (i.e. to 3.5 million)[2]. It has been estimated that demand in the UK private sector for elderly persons' housing for sale could be as high as 24,000 units per year[3].

It would therefore appear that this decade is witnessing the beginning of a boom in the provision of housing specifically for elderly people.

The next generation of this type of housing will, however, differ in many ways from previous examples. The main difference will be that the private sector (as owner-occupiers) will account for the majority of new schemes, with public rented sector provision declining in comparison. User expectations will be higher and more articulate as the market begins to benefit from a consolidation of experience and a wider choice.

Future residents will increasingly be born in this century: accustomed to the provisions of improved housing, education and welfare in comparison with their forebears, they will expect the comforts and necessities of our consumer age. Furthermore, the demographic profile of the occupants of this type of housing will shift towards the 'older elderly,' which will change the demands that will be placed upon the buildings and their management/services structure.

Management and funding, although always crucial, will become even more critical as private developers look to maintain profit margins and publicly funded or assisted projects seek to maintain levels of provision, but receive decreasing funding.

Although most developments have tended to be new buildings, the importance of siting implies inevitably that greenfield sites will quickly be eaten up and developed. Both private and public developers will invariably turn to re-using existing buildings or upgrading existing housing.

The goal posts have, therefore, moved, and will no doubt continue to move. This places a responsibility on both architects and developers not only to learn from the past but also to look forward and anticipate as far as possible future change and changing needs.

Aims of the book

This book is intended to be a practical handbook for both architects and their clients working together on designing housing for the elderly. It is concerned with design principles and so should apply to a whole range of extra-care and elderly person housing projects without the dogma of rigid design guidance which can so quickly become outdated.

With the first generation of built examples now some 30 years old, it offers the design professions a chance to take stock, evaluate past successes and failures, and thereby focus on how well user requirements and expectations have been met. It is an opportunity to update design criteria and to formulate a practical framework for planning or re-planning facilities to optimise functional suitability. This book owes a lot to the many years of work and dedication of housing associations and authorities who have commissioned and published research and, of course, to those architects who have produced many fine examples of housing for the elderly.

An important aim of this book, therefore, is to bring together material from various sources and illustrate through built examples, and to provide an information base directly applicable to the design of housing for the elderly. That is, not to supplant national codes or regulations, but rather to supplement them, with a view to describe activity-led design factors, so as to lead the designer or developer to understand *why* certain matters are important and not just *what* they are. The book has, therefore, been laid out to introduce the broad subject area first, and then to examine each major design element in detail. As with any building, each scheme will have its own virtues and deficiencies, and not everything in the photographic illustrations is necessarily to be commended; they should always be viewed with the recommendations of the text in mind.

1

The Building Types Defined

Almost as a reflection of its ever-changing and growing nature, the term 'housing for the elderly' can no longer relate specifically to one building type. Instead, it is best used as an umbrella term under which are housed a whole variety of buildings accommodating the elderly, which offer varying degrees of protection and support and aim to retain for them as far as possible a degree of independence and privacy.

Although similar building types have been developed in both the UK and the USA, the terminology differs. Definitions commonly used in both countries are therefore tabulated to show each country's language interpretations.

The United Kingdom

The then Ministry of Housing and Local Government's Circular 82/69 first divided into two categories what were then seen as the major developments in housing for elderly people.

Category One housing

Category One developments were intended for 'active elderly'. In self-contained bungalow type accommodation the residents were envisaged as maintaining a high degree of independence, being able to manage their own housework and even a small garden. Some types of retirement homes would fulfil a category one description (HTA categories are more recent and differ—see the end of this chapter).

Category Two Housing

This would normally consist of flats and have a much wider range of facilities, such as a common room and laundry. It was intended for less active old people who often lived alone and who needed smaller and labour-saving accommodation[1]. The designations category one and category two are still used in the United Kingdom to defined sheltered housing schemes, one may come across the term category one/two, meaning a hybrid of the two categories.

Residential care homes

These are sometimes referred to as part three homes, after that part of the National Assistance Act 1948, which first empowered local authorities to provide such facilities. Residential care homes usually take the form of single-room accommodation with communal dining and shared facilities for wc and bathroom. Residents will tend to require personal care assistance in the form of help with toilet, washing, dressing, and housework. Residents in need of personal care are not, therefore, ill or necessarily in need of medical supervision. Instead, as a result of increasing disability they have become unable independently to support themselves. Such accommodation has traditionally been provided by local authorities. However, very few new developments have been built during the past five years, and as a result there are often very long waiting lists for places in them.

Definitions of building type according to facilities and type of dwelling	United Kingdom								United States				
	Category I*	Category II*	Sheltered housing	Very sheltered housing	Retirement housing	Extra-care housing	Residential care homes	Nursing care homes	Independent housing units	Congregate housing	Personal care housing	Skilled nursing housing	Life-care communities
Self-contained bungalows or villas	●		●		●				●				●
Self-contained apartments	●	●	●	●	●	●			●	●			●
Single-bed units						●	●	●	●		●	●	●
Basic communal facilities (i.e. one lounge or laundry)	○	●	●		●				●				
Full communcal facilities (including central dining facilities)		○	●	●		●	●	●		●	●	●	●
Warden controlled alarm system	●	●	●	●	●	●	●	●	●	●	●	●	
On-site personal care facilities				●		●	●	●		○	●	●	●
On-site nursing care facilities						○		●				●	●

* These are *not* the same as the HTA categories on page 5

Recent years have, however, seen a large expansion in the number of privately funded residential homes.

Any home providing personal care to four or more elderly and dependent people within the private or voluntary sector is required under the Registered Homes Act 1984 to be registered with the local authority and to be open to regular inspections.

Nursing homes

Nursing homes provide accommodation, either short-stay or long-term, to those elderly suffering from a sickness, injury or infirmity. They provide nursing care by qualified nurses. Although the accommodation types vary, it is similar to that of the residential home. It is, however, the provision of nursing care as opposed to personal care which distinguishes this type of accommodation from residential homes. Any home providing nursing care to more than one person has, by law, to be registered with the local health authority and be open to regular inspections. Nursing homes have traditionally been developed within the private sector or with voluntary agencies and charities. However, some health authorities are now considering developing their own nursing homes as an alternative to the long-stay geriatric hospital wards.

Dual registration homes

The Registered Homes Act of 1984 also allowed for residential homes to be registered as nursing homes, being subject to inspection by both local councils and health authorities. The advantage of dual registration is that if a resident in a residential home becomes ill they may remain and be cared for within the same home, rather than having to move to a registered nursing home or hospital[2].

Sheltered housing

Perhaps the most commonly used term defining housing for the elderly, and includes the following three elements:
— A resident warden.
— An alarm system fitted to each dwelling.
— The occupancy of self-contained dwellings is restricted to the elderly[3].

Very sheltered housing

Essentially, very sheltered housing is an extension of conventional warden-controlled sheltered housing, but with a higher degree of input from welfare and personal care providers. The residential units may still be self-contained (i.e have their own kitchen and bathroom), but these units are intended primarily for the older or more frail elderly. Sometimes these types of accommodation are referred to as Category Two and a Half housing.

Retirement homes

A term used mainly in private sector developments for sale to the elderly, these are typically self-contained, sometimes detached residences, such as bungalows for the more active elderly. Increasingly, however, this term is beginning to embrace a wider range of facilities as the private sector expands its range of types.

Extra-care

This concept was developed by the Anchor Housing Association and provides facilities and a caring environment for those who have become too frail to cope with fundamental physical activities such as dressing, or getting out of bed, but are still relatively healthy and mentally stable. Although each resident may live independently, nursing and housekeeping support may also be provided as part of the extra-care. Organisations such as the Abbeyfield Society have also built their own extra-care developments.

The United States

Joe Jordan has described the building types that house elderly people in the United States.

Independent retirement housing units:

These are self-contained apartments designed for active or young elderly people. These will not always have any communal services, apart perhaps from the laundry. In urban and metropolitan areas they are usually mid-rise buildings: approximately eight storeys. Typically, their minimum size would be one hundred residential units. The more economic size would be about two hundred units, and the maximum three hundred. The economy of scale comes through the distribution of management services, purchasing and so forth. Public funding under the Federal 203 Program encouraged many developers throughout the USA. However, since its inception, funding has become scarcer. Today there is enormous competition for funding, with about one out of every ten projects being publicly funded. In recent years there has been a trend towards an integration between the development community and the sponsoring community, in order to accomplish further projects. In rural communities a similar type of housing has been sponsored, largely through the Farmers' Home Administration, and is usually single-family dispersed cottage-type housing. The scale of the units, because the communities are smaller, ranges from twenty-five to one hundred units.

Congregate housing

These developments provide some communal services in addition to the basic independent housing units. This housing includes communal areas, help with cleaning, shopping, and has communal dining facilities. It includes most types of assistance with independent living, short of direct personal care. Congregate housing demands a high level of servicing and staffing, so the management costs are higher. Such developments have therefore tended to be sponsored by church or charity organisations.

Personal care housing:

Whilst this type of housing has existed since the early 1960s it is only recently emerging in a different form, in that it is now almost entirely handled by the private sector. It is recognised that there is a need for personal care housing in which frailer or older elderly people can receive personal care and assistance with dressing, washing, etc. At one time such facilities were characterized by residents having to share bedrooms or bathrooms. However, as new government regulations have gradually come into force a new generation of this type of housing is now emerging with a minimum provision of single bedrooms with en-suite private bathroom, designed to mobility standards.

Skilled nursing home

This is the building type that cares for the elderly person in need of both personal and medical care and support. In the United States, because of reimbursement procedures which are governed by law, there are two types of facility: skilled nursing care and intermediate nursing care. In terms of the facility provision they are indistinguisable: the definition relates to the degree of medical supervision. Skilled nursing care involves supervision by a physician and intermediate nursing care involves supervision by a licensed nurse. The skilled nursing home is now developing as a major industry, moving from developments in the 1950s, which were small in scale and operated almost entirely as a cottage industry, to large organisations which may own fifty to a hundred nursing homes. Apart from a few charitable organisations, nursing homes are almost entirely funded within the private sector. Their size normally ranges from 120 beds, which is usually considered to be the minimum economic operating level, and increases in 60 units increments (based upon the number of beds per nursing station), with 240 bed units probably being the most economic to operate. The scale of the facility is very much tied to management practices which attempt to realise economies of scale through a consolidation of

experience, which ultimately benefits the consumer in terms of pricing levels.

Life care communities

This is the most recent and certainly the most sophisticated development in housing for elderly people and first started in the early 1960s. In 1984 it was estimated that there were over 600 life care communities in the USA[4]. One of the first such developments was built in the Philadelphia area by Quaker groups. In subsequent years a number of Quaker organisations, also in the Philadelphia area, sponsored similar facilities. During their first decade, therefore, life care communities were predominantly church-sponsored. However, in recent years the model has been taken up by the private sector. The normal population runs from 300 to 400 residential units. The facilities provided are usually divided into four types of unit.
1 Independent living: these tend to be bungalows or apartments for the active elderly.
2 Self contained apartments: these are combined with communal facilities to provide meals plus some social activities.
3 Personal care accommodation: this usually takes the form of single bedrooms with en-suite bathrooms and is intended for frailer, older elderly.
4 Nursing home facilities: the accommodation here would be similar to that of personal care, with the exception that medical supervision and care would also be available.

A common feature of life care communities is also to include a continuing care contract which covers the remainder of a resident's life. The ratio of self-contained apartments to nursing care units varies from one apartment per nursing care bed to just over four apartments per nursing care bed. This very much depends upon the management policy and market need of a particular location. Typically, the nursing care unit would have 60 beds.

At best, life care should be viewed as a concept rather than a defined building type. The concept is to enable one housing type (or types) to accommodate and service personal needs from active retirement, where support services would be mainly social and domestic, through to coping with both physical and mental frailty. This would then bring into play additional support including medical and personal care, all of which could be provided on site for the rest of a person's life.

Because of the flexibility that such a concept can offer for both residents and developers, the United States is now witnessing independent housing developments expanding their facilities to include nursing care accommodation, whilst at the same time nursing home operators are expanding their facilities to include independent living units.

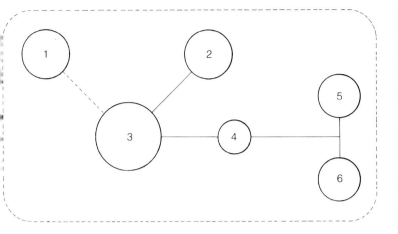

1. Independent living units: villas or bungalows set in grounds of life care campus.
2. Independent living units: apartments linked by corridors to communal facilities.
3. Communal facilities.
4. 'Outpatient' medical centre.
5. Personal care living units.
6. Nursing care living units.

As the need to promote more flexible building types to respond to the changing needs of the elderly has become more apparent, so the existing language of definition has become more outdated. Basically the degree of protection and support offered is the key to understanding the different types of accommodation that now exist.

The United Kingdom government Circular 82/69 of 1969 defined only two categories of care in sheltered housing. Since then there have been nearly two decades of continuous development, with the field being expanded to encompass at one end housing for pre-retirement active elderly through at the other end to housing for frail older elderly in need of 24 hour support nursing care. To move forward, therefore, we must leave behind the language of the past decades and formulate modes of definition more appropriate to projected future trends.

The old categories are redundant. They are completely out of touch with modern-day thinking and modern-day demands. The whole field of ageing and the elderly in terms of support care needs to be totally redefined. John White.

Help the Aged, an international charity dedicated to improving the quality of life for elderly people, in 1986 formulated seven categories which define the degree of support care throughout the aging process. This method of definition has been adopted in this book to provide a universal framework for describing the various buildings discussed.

HTA Category	Degree of support care
1	Non-specialised or adapted housing for active retired or pre-retired elderly who are completely able to live independently i.e. require no assistance with eating, hygiene, dressing, etc) and may therefore live in their own homes.
2	Housing for active elderly who may need some supervision but certainly can still look after themselves with a minimum of support. This may still include elderly who can remain in their homes after special adaptations have been made.
3	Purpose-built self-contained grouped accommodation for fit and active elderly, with the facilities for them to live substantially independently, but with 24 hour warden attendance. There would be a minimum of support or communal facilities.
4	Purpose-built self-contained grouped accommodation for physically frail but mentally alert elderly who do not need nursing care but may require occasional personal care supervision. Support facilities would include 24-hour warden attendance and provision of a cooked meal, but only as an option as and when required.
5	Physically alert but mentally frail who may require some personal care supervision. Communal facilities would be as for 4, but with additional support staff as required.
6	Residential care homes: purpose-built for elderly who may be mentally and physically frail and need personal care supervision. Many residents will be unable to support themselves independently. The accommodation therefore may not be self-contained. All meals will be prepared for residents and care staff may need to assist residents in bathing, eating, hygiene and dressing.
7	Nursing homes: as 6, except that residents may well be suffering from a sickness, injury or illness, either temporary or permanent. This would require licensed nursing/medical care. Accommodation would almost certainly be in single-bed units.

2

Why such Accommodation is Needed

Population changes

In September 1985 Age Concern published some basic facts about elderly people in the United Kingdom, providing a useful, demographic background to the need for housing for the elderly[1]. In 1981:

— The population of the United Kingdom was 55,767,381.
— Of this, 9,673,476 were over pensionable age (60 for women and 65 for men).
— 3,117,981 were aged 75 and over.
— 563,805 were aged 85 and over.
— 17.3% of the population of the United Kingdom were elderly people.
— A further increase of 3.3% in the elderly population is anticipated until 1991, when numbers will stabilise and eventually fall back.
— The proportion aged 75 and over will, however, increase by 27.6% and those aged 85 and over will increase by 79%.

As reported in 1986 in *Social Trends 16* (HMSO)[2], the number of people aged 65 or over is nearly five times greater now than it was in 1901. Since 1961 these numbers have grown by more than 2.0 million. However, the most significant increase is in those aged 85 and over, who are expected to make up more than one-tenth of the elderly by the year 2001.

In the United States the pattern is similar. Between 1953 and 1978 the elderly in the United States (those aged 65 years and over) grew twice as fast as the population as a whole. Some estimates indicate that by the year 2003 the elderly population will further increase by 59% as opposed to a total population rise of 28%[3].

In 1978 24.0 million people (11%) of the total population of USA were aged 65 or over. This figure is expected to rise to a projected 32.0 million by the year 2000 with a further projection rising to 55.0 million (18% of the population) by the year 2030[4].

As in the United Kingdom the most rapidly growing segment of the elderly group are those aged 85 years or over and they are expected to triple during the next 25 years.

Economic circumstances

The elderly, as will be discussed, are not a single socio-economic group. Elderly people are, however, over-represented among low income groups and those needing help from social and health services. Age Concern reported in 1985 that almost half of pensionable householders depended for at least 75% of their income on state pensions and benefits, and that many pensioners have to claim supplementary benefit because of their low income[5].

However, it is also true that there has been an improvement in pensioners' incomes and economic circumstances over the past 30 years. In comparison with those below pensionable age, in the United Kingdom in particular, pensioners are now retiring on incomes much nearer those they enjoyed in work than in the past. This is the result of higher state pensions, more occupational pension schemes and other social security benefits[6]. In the United States the poverty level amongst the elderly, whilst still a cause for acute concern, has declined over the past decade.

It is reported that the *per capita* income of the United States elderly actually exceeds that of many other age groups and that the disposable income of the elderly is greater than most segments of the population[7]. There is, therefore, a proportion of the elderly who are able and fortunate enough to buy themselves into a more suitable (or desirable) living environment. However, the need for suitable accommodation cuts right across the economic spectrum of the elderly, leaving others who are reliant upon public sector developments, for which funding is increasingly limited.

Housing suitability

As people grow older there is less likelihood that their home will be maintained or modernised. As children grow up and move away, so the family home quickly empties, becoming an increasing burden on its now elderly inhabitants. It becomes inconvenient to use, too large to heat and maintain and potentially dangerous as the ageing process inevitably restricts mobility.

The 1981 English House Conditions Survey showed that households in an unsatisfactory condition were more likely to be headed by an elderly person. The heads of the households of no less than 43% of unfit dwellings and 55% of dwellings lacking one or more basic amenity were aged 65 or over[8].

To this must be added the additional factor that older people will tend to spend more time at home. Through either not going out to work or disability, the home becomes far more the centre and in many cases the entirety of a person's experience of their world. The unsuitability of the home will, therefore, come into ever-sharper focus the more a person is bound by its walls.

For those previously in poor housing conditions in the rented sector, publicly funded or subsidised housing has a proud history of providing the elderly with a refuge in which to live their remaining years in good housing accommodation.

However, as government funding for public housing decreases in both the United States and the United Kingdom, so the problem will no doubt become more acute. This in turn will reinforce the importance of public sponsors and housing trusts in their search for alternative sources of funding for rented or subsidised accommodation for the less well-off elderly. The upturn in private housing developments does not, however, necessarily address itself to the plight of these elderly. Hence, the decrease in public funding projects should not be confused or linked with the take-up in the private sector, as in many ways they serve quite different ends of the housing market. Instead, it reflects the fact that more people are entering old age as owner-occupiers (50.7% in the United Kingdom, 80% in the United States).

For the new generation of elderly owner-occupiers this presents both new opportunities and very critical problems. Though it may have been unforeseen at the time, the postwar government incentives and aspirations to create a nation of owner-occupiers has led to a massive mismatch in housing suitability.

The potential of elderly person housing units for sale

Until comparatively recently there have been few alternatives available for the elderly owner-occupier. The factor deciding a move has tended to be a sudden or dramatic occurrence: for example an accident or an illness, severely restricted mobility, or the death of a spouse.

However, the option of buying a housing unit has opened up a relatively untapped market for those elderly who are fortunate enough already to own their own property and who wish to move to more suitable accommodation.

In 1983 the Housing Research Foundation in the United Kingdom commissioned the first of a series of research projects undertaken by the University of Surrey to investigate the market potential for sheltered housing units for sale[9] Their main conclusions included the following:

— The potential market for sheltered housing for sale to the retired is estimated at between 250,000 and 400,000 units.
— The rate of building for this market is estimated at 20,000 to 24,000 units per year.
— Sheltered housing for sale can be constructed throughout the United Kingdom to meet local demand.

Their first report related mainly to accommodation for the active elderly. Before 1983 fewer than 2,500 sheltered housing units for sale had been built. By the end of 1985 30,000 had been completed or were under construction. This today represents the fastest growing sector of the house-building market. It must be added that the market has existed for a number of years, but is only now being appreciated by builders and house developers.

In the United States the business community has also 'discovered' the elderly as a potentially lucrative and relatively untapped market. However, looking to future trends it is interesting to note that the research undertaken by the University of Surrey also points out:

It is predicted that in time the age distribution of residents will change and the average age [76 years in 1983] will be higher. This may lead to a greater number of more dependent residents who will make more demands on the warden/nursing services[10].

The third of their research studies, published in 1986, revealed:

Discussions with many of those involved in the development and management of retirement housing and with people living in such schemes have led us to believe that there is likely to be a significant demand for schemes which combine sheltered housing with health care facilities[11]. We believe that there is likely to be a significant demand for (such) continuing care schemes[12].

Therefore, reflecting the population shift, the need to develop suitable accommodation for the older elderly will become more significant as this building type assumes a more important role in the debate on housing for the elderly.

Staying put

Any move to specially designed accommodation must be seen against the background that many people will wish to remain in their homes for as long as they are physically or mentally able. But a disproportionately high number of older owners are found in older homes that remain unmodernised and without basic amenities, having inadequate heating and requiring major repairs. However, with government grant assistance there are agency and advice services such as Staying Put in the United Kingdom set up by The Anchor Housing Trust[13], which help elderly people improve and repair their properties. Purpose designed facilities cannot therefore be viewed as a panacea, providing suitable accommodation for all our elderly population, but rather as one in a series of options which ideally are based upon the free choice of each potential resident.

There is, therefore, real and increasing demand for a whole range of purpose-built housing accommodation for elderly people because:
— There are more elderly people (especially those aged over 85 years).
— Their present accommodation may no longer be suitable.
— There now exists an option, for those who own their own properties and have the means to realise their capital investment, to buy a dwelling and a package of support services specially geared to the elderly.
— However, a demand from lower-income elderly in the rented sector and those who are unable to buy into the market still exists, emphasising the crucial role that publicly assisted agencies will still need to perform.

3

Who are our Elderly People?

To try and define the needs of elderly people is like defining the needs of the human race, it's so vast. Pauline O'Driscoll.

Although one particular age can never serve as a universal watershed and represent the passing from middle to old age, it is commonly accepted that men over 65 years and women over 60 years, i.e. those who have become pensioners, may be defined as elderly. Many authorities further subdivide elderly people into younger old (up to 75–80 years) who are active and independent, and old-old (over 75–80 years), who are heavy consumers of care resources.

Therefore, without favour to class, status, wealth, culture, religion or race, the elderly are as diverse a cross-section of the population as any other group. The elderly age group can span more than 30 years, and thus include people with radically different life experiences, i.e. from those born in the 1890s to those in the 1920s, each representing an entirely dissimilar generation. Unless we die prematurely, we shall *all* become members of the elderly population.

Out of such diversity come both myths and gross generalisations about becoming older. This is largely because planners, agencies and legislators have attempted to define the needs of the elderly within a single framework. Instead, it must be recognised that the housing needs of the elderly are as diverse and complex as the elderly themselves. It is therefore important in any attempt to be sensitive to user needs to appreciate that such myths and generalisations are divorced from fact.

Dr Anne Roberts, a geriatrician with a special interest in the care of the elderly in the community, has explained that the process of ageing is often confused with ill-health. Normal ageing causes very little in the way of disability. People do become ill, but this is viewed as normal rather than treatable or preventable, simply because it is common. Just as at one time high infant mortality rates were viewed as normal because they were common, similarly our current attitudes will in future be considered primitive because of our assumption that the connection between ageing and disability is normal.

We have to assume that disability is due to ill health until proved otherwise. Dr Anne Roberts.

It is therefore important to adopt a more curative approach. For example, in assessing the needs of someone who is no longer mobile we should ask the question *why* a person can no longer walk, and whether this can be treated, rather than merely accept the condition as a consequence of old age.

However, the inevitability of the ageing process does bring into play the following factors which can potentially restrict one's life:

Inability to reach

The inability to reach such items as switches or shelves may be partly the result of a lack of dexterity in joints and nervous control of body movements. The fact that older people tend to be shorter than the rest of the population is also relevant. This may in part be explained by the fact that they are survivors of an earlier, less well-nourished generation. It is also true that the ageing process can cause a loss of up to 1½" in height. The 50th percentile of American men and women aged 65 to 75 years is estimated to be 1.697m (5 ft 7 in) and 1.565m (5 ft 1½ in) respectively[1].

Loss of reserve capacity of organs and systems

Elderly people become ill slowly, so their symptoms are difficult to detect; and once they do become ill they may need more help in recovering. This is where the ageing process becomes confused with illness. Unless the illness is diagnosed quickly, the condition which was potentially reversible can become irreversible.

Increased tendency to fall

Falls can be caused by from hazards outside the person (i.e. falling over a step); this can be prevented by sensitive design, which eliminates trip hazards and uses good lighting and contrasts in colour and texture. It is especially important for partially-sighted people that changes in level or direction are clearly indicated. Falls, however, can also result from illness inside the person, causing a sudden loss of balance or a collapse. This may initially highlight the importance of a good alarm system, with adequate service backup. However, as Dr Roberts points out, 'alarm systems are only useful when accessible after the accident. They rarely benefit that most vulnerable group, the mentally frail, who may find them difficult to use' (see chapter 7).

Decline in sensory input

With advancing age there is commonly some decline in one's ability to see or hear. The decline in sight necessitates sensitivity in the design of the built environment, the use of brighter lighting and visual contrast, and the provision of signs, notice boards and clocks which can be easily read. That means that any signage should be adequately large with contrasting print, and should be set low enough to allow for the generally short stature of the elderly population.

The decline in hearing implies attention to the design of the acoustic environment, as radios and televisions will tend to be set by many residents at a higher volume (see chapter 7). From a medical point of view, a curative approach to sight and hearing problems, often remediable, will also help.

Maintaining body temperature

The ability to maintain body temperature becomes more difficult as we grow older. The importance of providing adequate heating through the year therefore becomes critical. A common contributory cause of death among elderly people is hypothermia, in which the body temperature drops to an abnormally low level. Any heating system must therefore compensate for this additional loss of body heat and provide a comfortable, reliable and draught free environment.

Incontinence

Incontinence is not normal and may well be a symptom of another condition, such as dementia or depression. It can also be caused by the inability to find a toilet when required. A tendency towards incontinence can therefore be aggravated by poor location of toilets: for example by the need to negotiate a flight of stairs or a long walk down a corridor. This in turn can lead to anxiety and depression.

Immobility

Though many elderly people remain independent, mobility problems are very common as the result of stiffening joints or a fall. Many elderly people will, through the process of time, be prone to spend periods either wheelchair or bed-bound.

However, it is important not to lose sight of the fact that there are just as many disabled young people as there are diabled over retirement age. There is no justification for restricting design for the handicapped only to housing developments for the elderly.

Mental frailty

Dr Anne Roberts defines the term 'frail' as being that state in which all possible treatment of any disability has been carried out but a residual disability remains. She has also explained that it is not normal, i.e. part of the ageing process, to become mentally impaired. Only a slight and insignificant decline in memory which would have started at the age of 15 years would be expected. Even of the older elderly, i.e. those aged over 80 years, four out of five can expect to suffer no significant loss of mental ability.

Normal elderly people are mentally alert adults, *fully able to take charge of their own lives and should be treated as such. Dr Anne Roberts.*

The process of ageing should not automatically be seen as a period of potential physical deterioration. Furthermore, even deterioration in one's physical functions does not necesarily lead to and should not be confused with mental disability. Dr M. Powell Lawton.

Despite this, mental frailty remains a major factor among the disabilities of elderly people. Whilst the loss of sight, hearing and the ability to keep warm can all be alleviated by improving the quality and technology of the building fabric, sensitivity to mental frailty is a more complex and subtle matter.

Mental function in elderly people is most commonly impaired by:
— Dementia
— Confusion
— Depression

Dementia

This can take two forms. The first involves the condition known as Alzheimer's disease, which causes profound mental deterioration and can occur from 50 years onwards. The condition is more common in women than men. Over one million Americans suffer from this disease. The second type is related to blood-vascular conditions and is more common in men then women, occurring more about the age of 70 years.

Common symptoms of dementia are:
— Loss of memory and the ability to think clearly.
— Loss of ability to make judgements.
— Loss of inhibitions, e.g. performing private functions in public.
— Loss of emotional function and control (people who have been caring, loving people become greedy, selfish and aggressive).
— Loss of ability to make if/then connections, e.g. 'If I drop a lighted cigarette on the carpet then that could start a fire'.
— Wandering (which can be a combination of loss of memory and a subconscious urge to escape from an intolerable situation).

Whilst sadly dementia is not curable, a well-designed environment and well-organised care can improve the quality of life of the sufferer considerably. Dr Anne Roberts.

People need to maintain their individual identity, so this is where architects can play a positive role in allowing sufficient space for people to have the choice to surround themselves with their own possessions. A wardrobe or a chest of drawers are such possessions, that can provide an invaluable link with the past and reality. *Pauline O'Driscoll.*

A move to a new environment commonly worsens the mental state. In general, mentally frail people who become unable to remain in their own homes tend to be more suited to facilities that offer extra care rather than to sheltered or congregate envirements.

The lack of a routine can also aggravate a failing memory. Elderly people will tend not to go out to work, and therefore have more time on their hands during their retirement years.

On the whole, women tolerate this better because their lifestyle changes less; you wake up on your sixtieth birthday and still there is the washing up to do. For a man used to a lifetime of work outside the home environment, he loses his structured day, his perception of his place in society.
Dr Anne Roberts.

External cues to reintroduce some form of routine are therefore important. Dr Roberts recommends to housing managers that they should shape each day by some form of activity: i.e. Monday, luncheon clubs; Tuesday, bingo, etc. the important factor is to provide a contrast between one day and the next. Without this it is possible for anyone with the slightest tendency to mental frailty to lose track of the hours and days and slip into confusion.

The importance of being able to live in an environment which contains stimulation and variety is also seen by Dr M. Powell Lawton as a crucial factor in the psychological well being of a resident.

A very important aspect of older people living alone is the maximizing of the amount of information and control that can be obtained from a very small proximate environment. Our research has taught us that one of the most basic aspects of the person/environment relation is that the environment is the source of knowledge that is relevant to how a person behaves.

All kinds of factors may impose limitations on how much a person can learn from the environment. For example, when a person retires, a large potential environment learning sector is blotted off, and as one becomes confined to a building and then perhaps to a room, so this limitation process continues.

This focuses on the importance of the designed internal environment, as this is where the greatest proportion of the continued learning experience is going to take place. This in turn brings into play why places of activity and not tranquility should be designed into projects. Dr M. Powell Lawton.

Housing for elderly people should look outward, literally and metaphorically, and opportunities for physical activity and mental stimulation should be as far as possible designed into that environment.

Confusion

Confusion occurs when a person appears to become out of touch with their surroundings and becomes forgetful or unable to manage their own affairs. Reversible causes of confusion can be mistaken for dementia; they include the effects of drugs and illnesses such as anaemia and infections, and dietary deficiencies. These can all be factors which can contribute to making a person's mental condition appear worse than it is, and which should respond to medical treatment.

Depression

True depressive illness is common in old people: its rate of occurrence may be as high as 10%. It is, however, sometimes difficult to distinguish those who are dementing from those who are suffering from depression. It is important to distinguish the two, because depression is treatable.

However, as Dr Roberts points out, we have to separate depressive illness, which is abnormal and needs treating, from the various causes of becoming sad, which are quite normal. For example, mourning, that is grieving for people and things you have lost, is a normal part of life.

Depression may result from 'learned helplessness' and the inability to influence what happens to you. It is therefore healthier for older people to maintain as much self-determination as possible. Dr Anne Roberts.

Whatever age you are, you feel what you feel, and the need to be able to cry and be able to grieve is all part of respecting an individual and maintaining their sense of self. Frustration can also lead to depression as one's choices can begin to close down, even to the point that even if you want to get up to go to the other end of the room it can no longer be carried out as a spontaneous action, it has to be thought about. Pauline O'Driscoll.

Despite the restrictions of ageing, our basic human needs and desires remain. It should never be presumed, for example, that elderly people are not sexually active. Architects should be aware of all these factors, creating an environment which does not contribute to or aggravate restrictions, but instead gives unobtrusive support, making it possible to maintain a lifestyle in privacy, dignity and without undue dependence.

Therefore, given the right support, elderly people can still live as normal lives as the level of backup services and the correct environment will allow.

We have to hold a vision of older people, even if they are in a very decrepit state and dementing, as having value and purpose. Pauline O'Driscoll.

4

An Historical Perspective

In order to understand the current situation and to be able to project a possible future it is important first to place into perspective past experience in housing for the elderly and briefly to trace its origins.

In both the United States and the United Kingdom, housing specially built for the elderly has its origins in church and charity. This philanthropic tradition of providing shelter for the elderly has been continued through by government funding and public sponsorship. However, it is only comparatively recently that housing for the elderly has been provided by the private sector, and this has led to a dramatic shift in the emphasis and image of housing for elderly people.

Pre-history: the first one thousand years

The first known built example of supportive accommodation, specially built for elderly people, dates back to the earliest known almshouse in England in 939 AD. Almshouses were at first provided by the church and tended to be self-contained dwellings grouped around a courtyard and sited next to church buildings. More were built during the eleventh and twelfth centuries.

During the sixteenth century, when the influence and position of the church as provider diminished, almshouses contined to be developed but were funded by wealthy philantropists. Accommodation was often provided rent-free, with a gift of coal.

The first generation of housing for the elderly therefore relied upon the goodwill and charity of the church and worthy citizens. The accommodation was provided for those elderly who were poor and would be otherwise without a home or, later, would have been condemned to an existence in a workhouse. Because of poor housing conditions and the almost total lack of medical care, survival into old age must have been viewed as extraordinary, even up to the last century. It was not until the beginning of this century that the Royal Commission on the Poor Law in 1909 acknowledged and recommended the provision of special housing for the elderly.

State funded provision

After the Second World War the setting up of a welfare state for the United Kingdom embodied the earlier recommendations for housing the elderly under sheltered conditions. With the help of government legislation, some county councils began to build sheltered housing units, which were mainly one- or two-storey cottage-style developments.

As *The Architects' Journal* of 18 January 1951 reported:

Many local authorities are now paying attention in their housing plans to the special needs of the elderly[1]

Almshouses, Barnet, Hertfordshire, UK, sixteenth century. Almshouses are the first known built example of housing designed specially for the elderly. They were characteristically self-contained cottage-style units arranged around a courtyard.

ABS Homes, Frenchlands Hatch, East Horsley, Surrey, UK, 1958. Architects: Clifford Culpin & Partner, for Architect's Benevolent Society Homes Trust, (photo by Sydney W. Newbery). One thousand years after the first almshouses, the winner of an architectural competition retains the concept of a courtyard with cottage style units. The development consists of self-contained one and two bedroom units, together with a warden's house. The layout of the bedroom allows for double doors to open onto the living room to provide for flexibility of the space, especially for those confined to bed. This was innovative for 1958 and it is only recently that more schemes are now including this feature.

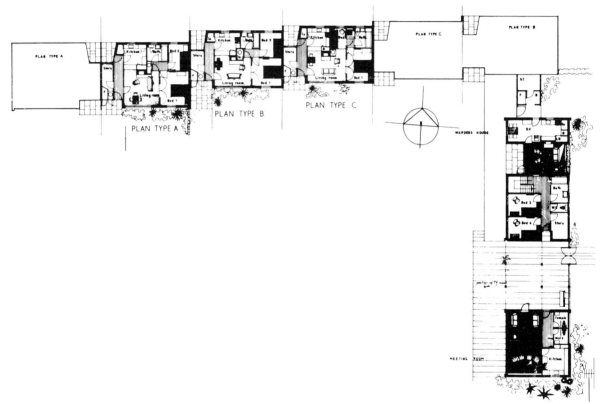

Stoneleigh Court, Clayhall, Ilford, Essex, UK, 1956. Architects: Ilford County Council, now Redbridge Architect's Department. Ilford was among the first local authorities to embark upon a programme of sheltered housing. At Stoneleigh Court the communal hall overlooks the adjacent residential area and the development was designed to be a part of the local environment.

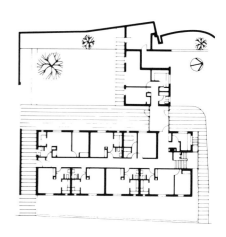

Elizabeth Court, Aldeburgh, Suffolk, UK, 1965. Architects: Peter Barefoot for Aldeburgh Borough Council. (Photo by John Pantlin). An L-shaped building facing the High Street, with a combination of bed-sits and one bedroom flats. There is also accommodation on the first floor, but as was usual for this period no lift was included.

Stonald Road, Whittlesey, Suffolk, UK, 1977. Architects: Matthew Robotham Associates for Nene Housing Society. (Photo Matthew Robotham Asssociates).

Key
1 Warden's house.
2 Common room.

In 1958 the Ministry of Housing and Local Government published its first *Design Bulletin* and throughout the 1960s and 1970s further government guidelines were published, setting down standards in design, layout and specification. This, however, ceased in 1981 when all Housing Circulars affecting local authority housing provision were withdrawn.

Housing association provision

The 1960s saw a rapid growth in the development of housing associations, which became eligible for subsidies in providing accommodation for the elderly. Local authority and housing associations provided the majority of housing units for elderly people during the succeeding 20 years. This second generation of sheltered housing, which was almost entirely for rent and not for sale, was based upon planned provision, either directly or indirectly via government subsidy. The occupants of such schemes tended to come from the lower income groups and from previously rented accommodation. The children of these elderly were, however, meanwhile establishing the post-war British trend towards home ownership, and thereby setting in train the pattern for the next generation of sheltered housing.

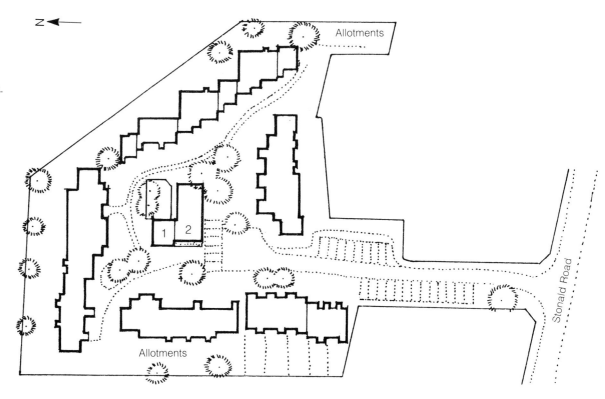

Stonald Road: a mixed development of 12 × one person bungalows, 20 one-person and 16 two-person flats sited within a residential area. Accommodation is on two floors with staircase access. This was built to government recommended standards. Even during the 1970s the emphasis remained on facilities for the active elderly in UK sheltered housing. Also includes 1 five-person warden's house, 5 five person houses with garage, and a common room. 26 car spaces in all.

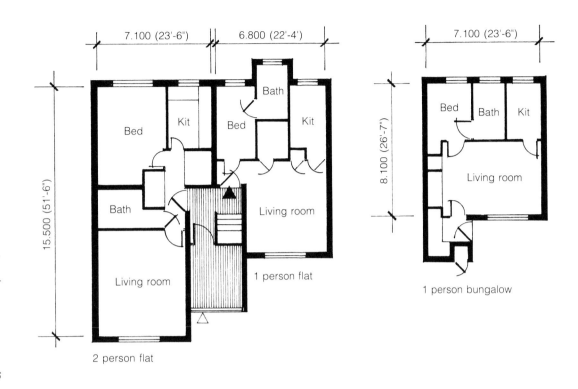

7.100 (23'-6")   6.800 (22'-4')

7.100 (23'-6")

15.500 (51'-6")

8.100 (26'-7")

Bed   Kit   Bed   Bath   Kit

Bath   Living room

Living room

2 person flat

1 person flat

Bed   Bath   Kit

Living room

1 person bungalow

Vicarage Road, Enfield, UK. Architects: Michael Twigg Brown & Partners. 1984, for The Anchor Housing Association. (Photo by Robert Wilkinson).
A scheme of 32 flats plus warden's house designed during the early 1980s, and representing the shift in emphasis towards more design considerations for the older elderly. Facilites also include an elevator to the upper floors and at least one flat designed for wheelchair access. The external appearance of the building may also be recognised as typical of the type of sheltered housing developments during this period in the United Kingdom.
2 person flat
1 person bungalow

Ground floor plan

At Mount Pleasant Lane, London, U.K. Anthony Richardson & Partners have responded to an inner city site surrounded by a nondescript estate of middle rise flats by providing a clear contrast. The use of external materials, when viewed in the general context of the site and its environs, certainly has the effect of giving a lift to the area and has become a landmark to the local community. Residents also like the fact that it does not look like 'an old people's home', but rather 'a posh hotel'. For Newlon Housing Trust. Photo: Martin Charles.

Housing for older people as a generic architectural form, despite a general tendency towards a rather bland domestic imagery, has more recently produced buildings of architectural excellence in a variety of styles.

Crisp lines and contrasting use of materials adds light and variety to Tuckers Court, Peterborough, U.K. by Mathew Robotham Associates, for the Minster General Housing Association Ltd. Photo: Bush Photographic.

The courtyard concept of the earlier almshouses interpreted with a fine attention to architectural detail and scale by Sidell Gibson Partnership at Atwater Court, Lenham, Kent, U.K., for The English Courtyard Association. Photo: Steve Stephens Photography.

Privately funded provision

Towards the end of the 1970s, local authority expenditure on housing decreased and funding for housing associations also became harder to obtain. About this time, there was a growing realisation that more people than ever before were reaching retirement age as owner-occupiers. In 1976 a consultation paper by the DOE and DHSS actually advocated the encouragement of privately financed developments of sheltered housing which would be for sale rather than rent[2].

Indeed, a small family-run building company, McCarthy & Stone, were already building a development of sheltered accommodation for sale; many housing developers and organisations credit McCarthy & Stone with spotting the market. Within five years of its first development in 1977, McCarthy & Stone became the market leader in the private sector.

The Baker and Parry reports, first published in 1983, for the Housing Research Foundation[3] which first identified the demand for private sector units for sale, can be seen as further encouraging expansion in the United Kingdom private sector market in sheltered housing. This third generation of housing for elderly people was therefore very much geared to those who had the financial means to buy themselves into suitable accommodation.

The United States

As in the United Kingdom, building new housing for elderly people had been associated with the needs of lower-income groups. This had traditionally required subsidy through government funding in the form of low interest loans, or appreciations by charitable sponsors. One of the oldest facilities can be traced to the eighteenth century in Philadelphia, where the church provided refuge for elderly people giving shelter, food and clothing. Further charitable organisations developed in the nineteenth century providing accommodation and a degree of help and support.

The 1950s saw the first Federal state conference on ageing, but it was not until the early 1960s that a small number of housing units designed for elderly people began to appear, funded by the Department of Health, Education and Welfare (HEW).

A Federal government funded housing programme (the 203 Housing Program) also encouraged non-profit-making organisations such as churches and other benefit society groups to develop housing for elderly persons. The type of accommodation was basically for active elderly and contained a minimum of communal and support facilities. Throughout the 1960s and 1970s the private sector began to develop large-scale housing communities, primarily in the sun belt areas, again geared towards the active elderly. Sun City in Arizona is probably the most well-known example.

The need to provide additional care facilities in the form of congregate housing was, however, first recommended to Congress by President Kennedy in 1963. It was not until 1978, however, that legislation was passed to allow for sufficient government subsidies to encourage a small number of congregate developments to get under way.

The number of publicly-sponsored housing programmes for elderly people is likely to decline in the United States as funding becomes more limited. The private sector, again serving a different market, has however recently expanded and has recognised the need to offer a whole range of accommodation and facilities to cater for both active and frail elderly.

Despite the relatively recent appearance of extra care and congregate housing, the majority of new developments built during the past 30 years have been designed almost exclusively for the active elderly. This legacy of the recent past will, however, leave future generations to inherit a building stock which may well become redundant in terms of its functional suitability, because of the inevitability of the process of ageing. The next generation of housing for elderly people must aim at buildings that can more easily adapt and change to meet the increasing constraints of the ageing process over time.

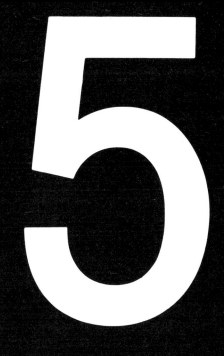

The Building Types Compared

This section provides a walk-through sample of the various types of accommdation for elderly people which have been completed in the past eight years. The buildings will be compared and analysed in terms of site location, design layout and space standards. If it is possible to characterize the building types in terms of the facilities and the level of support they offer, then this method of analysis makes an important step towards identifying the type of market and need to which a particular development should aim to respond.

Fullwell Court

Great Linford, Milton Keynes, UK
Completed 1985
For: Anchor Housing Association
Architects: The Tooley and Foster Partnership
HTA category: 3/4/5

Great Linford is a recently developed local centre, being part of the New Town of Milton Keynes. The immediate neighbourhood is primarily newly-built residential, two-storey family housing.

Funding
Anchor Housing Association subsidised via the Housing Corporation. Flats offered on a rental basis only.

Number and type of dwellings
38 two-person one-bedroom flats
1 two-person one-bedroom flat for wheelchair use.

Area of typical dwelling
41m^2 (441 sq. ft.)

Management
Anchor Housing Association.

Number of storeys.
Ground plus first.

Location/access
Close to local shopping facilities and community centre. Off-street parking for 13 cars. Covered canopy by dining room and wheelchair user's flat.

Facilities for the disabled
General circulation areas to mobility standards. Lift access to the first floor accommodation. All

Site plan.

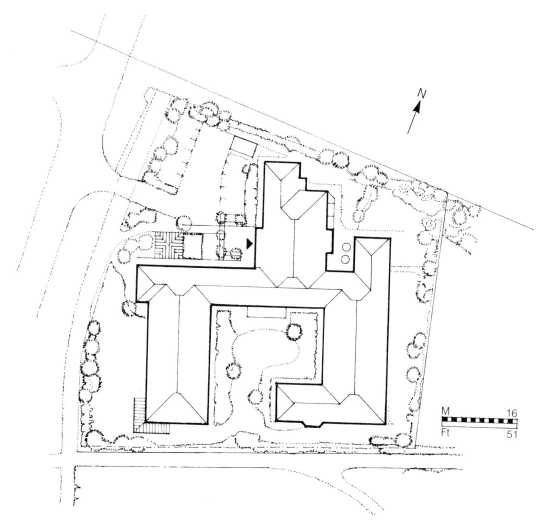

Fullwell Court view into main entrance.

Ground floor plan.

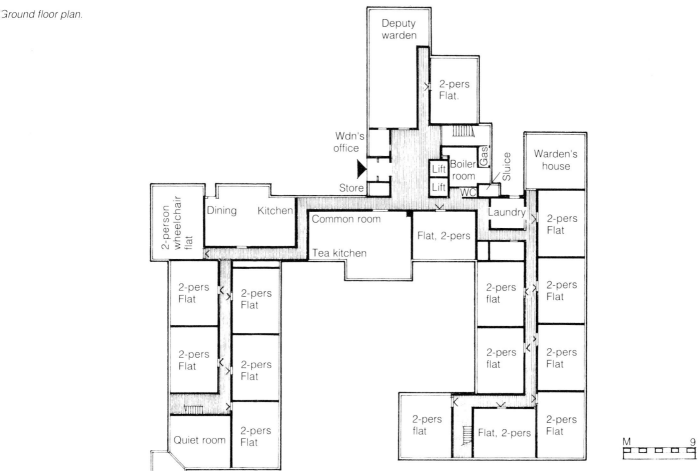

Deputy warden

2-pers Flat.

Wdn's office

Store

Lift

Lift

Boiler room

Gas

Sluice

WC

Warden's house

2-pers Flat

2-person wheelchair flat

Dining

Kitchen

Common room

Tea kitchen

Flat, 2-pers

Laundry

2-pers Flat

2-pers Flat

2-pers Flat

2-pers flat

2-pers Flat

2-pers Flat

2-pers Flat

2-pers flat

2-pers Flat

Quiet room

2-pers Flat

2-pers flat

Flat, 2-pers

2-pers Flat

Conservatory

M 9

The conservatory has proved popular with many of the residents and allows the opportunity of indoor gardening all the year round.

Interior of bedroom. The problem of fitting residents' existing furniture into flats is common to many developments.

First floor plan.

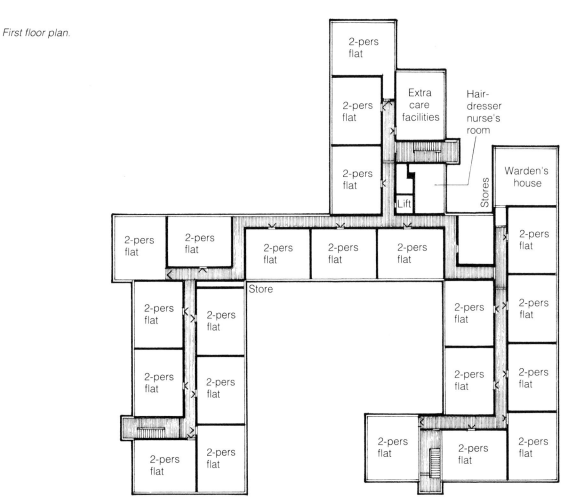

flats are to mobility standards. A two-person flat on the ground floor designed to wheelchair standards. One disabled user WC on ground floor.

Heating
Gas central heating from central boiler. Hot water all supplied from central point.

Communal facilities
Common room.
Quiet room.
Hairdressing/hobbies room.
Guest room.
Conservatory.
Dining room/kitchen.

Warden accommodation
Warden's house plus deputy warden's flat.

Special facilities
An extra care service base located on the first floor to serve as a base from which additional support (assisted washing, laundry service or cleaning of apartment and help with meal preparation) can be given to frail tenants according to their needs.

Comments
Fulwell Court is designed to accommodate a proportion of less active elderly people. Residents can reach the communal facilities and other dwellings along heated corridors, yet they may still live independently. This was Anchor's first extra care scheme. Although designed as a conventional sheltered housing project, it does include the extra facilities and more staff than usual, to allow for a number of frail elderly people to be accommodated. The extra care unit includes a separate assisted bath and shower and a room for day care staff. Arrangements have been made with the local social services to provide a special team of care professionals to offer a total of 100 hours a week to those tenants who need help with dressing, hygiene and meals. This unit, by acting as a service base, provides an in-built flexibility to the scheme in that a resident does not necessarily have to move out or change flats. Instead, the input of domestic and medical services is simply adjusted to changing needs.

5.550 (18'-1")

Store
Hall
Bath
Bedroom
Kitchen
Living room

7.500 (24'-8")

Typical two person flat layout. Note the only internal room is the bathroom.

The main common room opens out to the south facing courtyard.

Interior of living room.

General view of the two rehabilitated blocks. The semi-circular arcade forms the main entrance to the new communal building. This in turn connects the two high-rise apartment towers which have been completely renovated for elderly occupancy.

Wilson Park

Philadelphia, Pennsylvania, USA
Completed 1984
For: Philadelphia Housing Authority
Architects: Jordan Mitchell Inc. with Wallace Roberts and Todd
HTA category: 3/4/5

Wilson Park lies to the south of Philadelphia city centre. The area suffers from poor housing conditions. The high rise blocks were originally designed and used for public housing family units in 1952. However, these fell into disrepair and became vacant in 1977. The architects were commissioned to convert the high rise blocks and to provide communal facilities for use by local elderly residents.

Funding
Federal Office of Housing and Urban Development (HUD). Flats are rented to residents on a subsidised system, under which the rent is determined by each resident's ability to pay.

Number and type of dwellings
140 one-bedroom two-person flats (including 14 for wheelchair users).

Area of typical dwelling
59m^2 (630 sq. ft.)

Management
Philadelphia Housing Authority.

Number of storeys
Ground plus eleven storeys.

Location/access
Surrounded by 260 public housing units. There is level access to the site. General stores within walking distance. Off-street parking for 17 plus cars. Parking also available adjacent to the site.

Facilities for the disabled
General circulation areas and dwelling units designed to mobility standards. Elevator to all floors.

Heating
Central boiler gas-fired central heating system with individually controllable radiators. Hot water also centrally supplied.

Communal facilities
Sitting lounge.
Dining hall.
Laundry.
Outside sitting area.
Warden accommodation. No resident warden, but 24 hour on site attendance by supervisor/security officer. Housing manager's office and staff adjacent to development which also handles other public housing in the immediate area.

Special facilities
Lounge and dining area is also used by elderly non-residents in the area. The dining hall supports multiple use, as a meeting room and for general entertainments including the showing of films. A medical room is used by visiting practitioners (mainly chiropodists). The entrance with its semi-circular canopy is a popular vantage point used by residents for observing the comings and goings of the building.

Comments
Although Wilson Park was originally designed as family units, its conversion and use for elderly residents perhaps provides a useful pointer to many similar inner urban situations. Residents appear to prefer being 'off the ground' for security reasons and enjoy the views over Philadelphia. The nature of high-rise implies vertical as opposed to horizontal circulation space. Whilst this does reduce the length of corridors, it can also reduce those opportunities for social contact associated with corridors, which can function as a street. At Wilson Park, therefore, the design requires residents to pass through the lounge area to reach the elevators to the apartments. This is done with an eye to the potential problems of isolation that have been associated with high-rise in general housing.

Site plan. Part of the conversion programme included new elevators and wider doorsets to accommodate wheelchair users. The fabric of the blocks was also upgraded to improve sound and thermal insulation and to minimize maintenance.

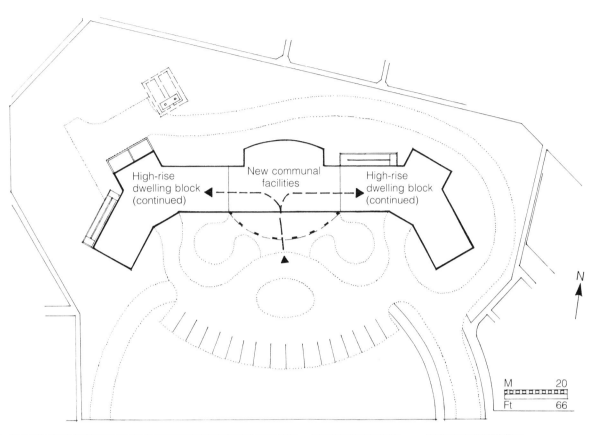

Canopy. Around 5 o'clock in the afternoon, non-residents begin to assemble for their evening meal with residents inside the building.

The security booth. Because of the security problems of this area, each visitor has to sign when they enter and leave the building.

The sitting areas. Many residents pass the time of day simply sitting in the lounge area and this being adjacent to the dining room brings with it the opportunity of becoming a major social centre within the development.

Interior of typical kitchen. All units have high standards of kitchen and bathroom facilities. 14 of the units are designed specifically for wheelchair use.

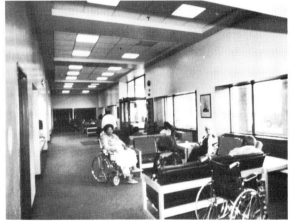

Plan of the communal area.

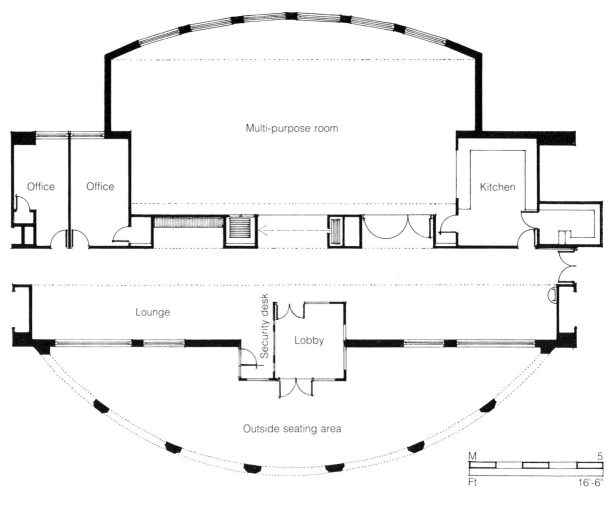

Office

Office

Multi-purpose room

Kitchen

Security desk

Lounge

Lobby

Outside seating area

M ⊢─┤ ⊢─┤ ⊢─┤ 5
Ft ───────────────── 16'-6"

Plan of typical dwellings. Clustering of units around a central core in high-rise developments does allow for double daylight aspect but the corridor as street is lost as an opportunity for social contact.

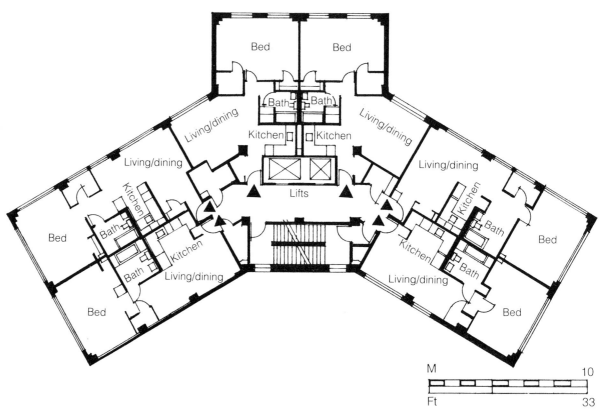

Bed

Bed

Bath Bath

Living/dining

Living/dining

Kitchen Kitchen

Living/dining

Living/dining

Lifts

Bed

Kitchen

Bath

Kitchen

Bath

Kitchen

Bath

Bed

Kitchen

Bath

Living/dining

Living/dining

Bed

Bed

M ⊢──┤⊢──┤⊢──┤⊢──┤ 10
Ft ───────────────────── 33

Manston Court

Lord's Hill, Southampton, Hampshire, UK
Completed 1982
For: Southampton City Council
Architects: Southampton City Council Architects'
Department, project architect David Bull
HTA category: 3/4/5

Lord's Hill is Southampton's last area of major
housing development. It comprises a mixture of
low cost private and council homes occupying a
semi-rural location about four miles from the city
centre. The site lies just outside the main district
centre at Lord's Hill. It was a conscious decision
of Southampton Council to site the development
in a neighbourhood which would be characterised by young families.

Funding
Southampton City Council (Housing Committee),
with asistance from Hampshire Social Services
Department and Area Health Authority. Flats are
rented from the City Council.

Number and type of dwellings
58 one-bedroom flats.
2 two-bedroom flats.

*View to main
entrance of Man-
ston Court.*

*Typical floor plan
(first).*

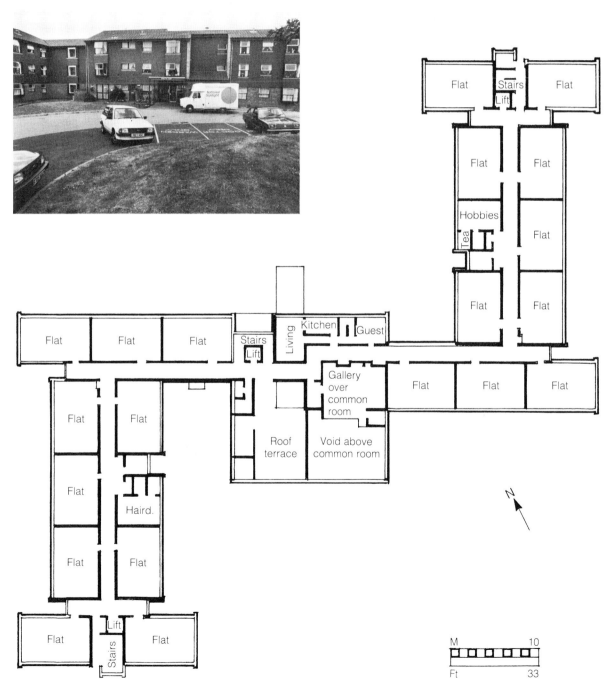

Entrance canopy by main entrance. This includes an entry-phone system. The threshold has also been carefully designed to provide a level barrier-free entrance in and out of the building.

Area of typical dwelling
42m² (451 sq. ft.)

Management
Southampton City Council Housing Department.

Number of storeys
Ground plus two storeys.

Location/access
Manston Court is within walking distance of Lord's Hill district centre with its shopping facilities, including a hypermarket, shopping parade, health centre, library, public house and church. Buses also connect Lord's Hill to Southampton city centre.

Facilities for the disabled
As a scheme intended for use by less active elderly people, all circulation areas are designed to mobility standards. Also, as smoke detectors and dispersal units are used, the doors do not have to be fire rated or self closing. Each floor is serviced by three lifts and all communal areas are reachable by heated corridors.

Heating & hot water
Electric under-floor heating with central boiler for hot water.

Communal facilities
Common room/dining room.
Residents bar.
Hobbies room.
Upper common room.
Roof terrace/patio.
Hairdressing room.
Quiet room/library.

Warden accommodation
One warden's flat, plus two bed-sitting flats used only for sleeping-in when the staff are on call outside normal hours; the two flats are used on a rota by four other members of staff.

Special facilities
Each residential wing includes a stack of special units such as doctors' consulting rooms and

Typical flat layout.

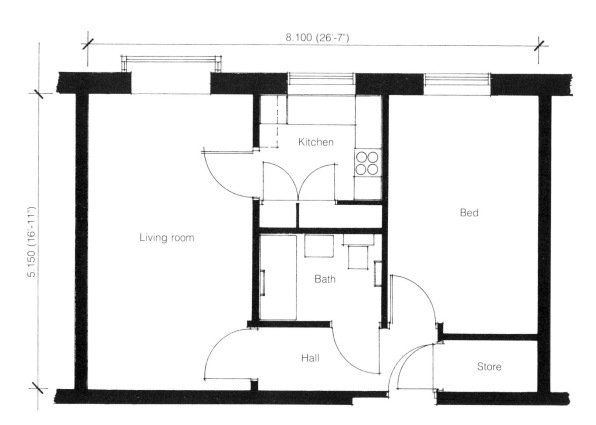

One of the main successes in the communal facilities at Manston Court is the self-financing licensed bar situated in the common room.

chiropodist's room. There are also laundry facilities. The large kitchen serving the dining room, like the other communcal facilities, can provide for a community larger than that of the residents alone: it is a long-term aim to make these available to elderly people in the area who may be living in their own homes or in more traditional sheltered housing which lacks this provision.

Comments
Manston Court is designed to accommodate older elderly people. However, they are expected to be mobile enough to move around without assistance, to be continent and able to dress and to be sufficiently alert mentally to orientate themselves. Therefore, while the basic layout of the scheme very much follows a conventional type of sheltered housing, Manston Court is designed as very sheltered housing because of the level of health and social services input available to each resident. From the outset, Manston Court was planned by a health care planning team for the elderly, which included representatives from the health and social services and city council department. A team approach is adopted towards the care and monitoring of each resident, and the building can adapt to both the active and frail elderly simply by an adjustment in the type of care a resident will require throughout their stay.

Common room with gallery over. Some residents prefer to sit in the gallery and observe the activities in the main common room.

Interior of kitchen.

Gallery seen from common room.

The roof terrace provides a sheltered and accessible outdoor space for all residents.

Hairdressing room. Each resident's wing includes a stack of special units of standard size rooms which vary in function from floor to floor. Other similar sized rooms are used by visiting chiropodists, doctors and nurses.

General view of Golda Meir House.

Golda Meir House

Newton, Massachusetts, USA
Completed 1979.
For: Jewish Community Housing for the Elderly,
Boston. (With assistance from Federal Office of
Housing and Urban Development).
Architects: Larkin Glassman and Prager; project
architect: Mayo Larkin.
HTA category: 3/4/5

Newton is a suburb west of Boston: an area of
mainly middle to upper income low-rise family
houses. The development itself is in an almost
rural setting, adjacent to open countryside and a
local golf course.

Funding
Federal Office of Housing and Urban Development (HUD) under Section 8 Housing. Units are
offered to rent and rents are subsidised in relation
to the amount each resident can pay.

Number of type of dwellings
Total 125 units including 5 two-bedroom flats and
120 one-bedroom flats (of which 10 are currently
fitted out for wheelchair/disabled users with
special kitchen and bathroom details and facilities).

Area of typical dwelling
49m^2 (528 sq ft) for one-bedroom flats.
66m^2 (708 sq ft) for two-bedroom flats.

Mangement
The Jewish Community Housing for the Elderly,
which is a non-profit organisation which also
manages four other similar developments.

Number of storeys
Ground plus five storeys.

Location/access
Golda Meir House is not located directly adjacent
to local facilities. To compensate for this, there is
a small shop within the development and for
those residents who do not drive there are pick-
up facilities run by the management agency who
are also able to take residents to city centre and
shopping facilities. There is also an adjacent
metro trolley system to Boston city centre, which
offers reduced fares to senior citizens.

Site layout.

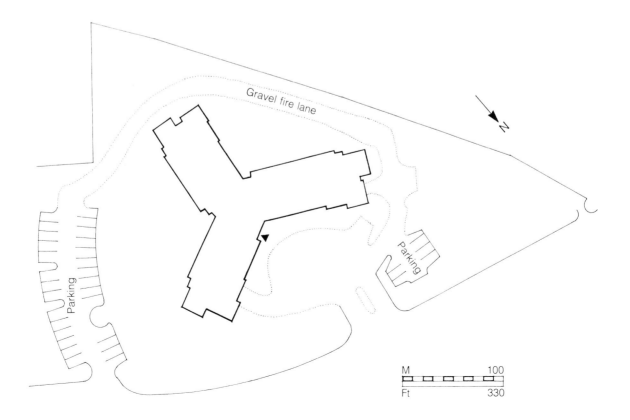

Disabled car user's space clearly defined.

From the reception desk the main communal facilities are just off the corridor, and have glass shop-type fronts like those of a normal street.

The dining room is not only where people eat, it also is used throughout the day for residents to meet, to play cards. More than any other of the communal spaces, the dining room is a major social centre of this development.

Living room of typical flat.

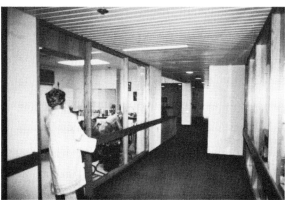

Layout at ground floor.

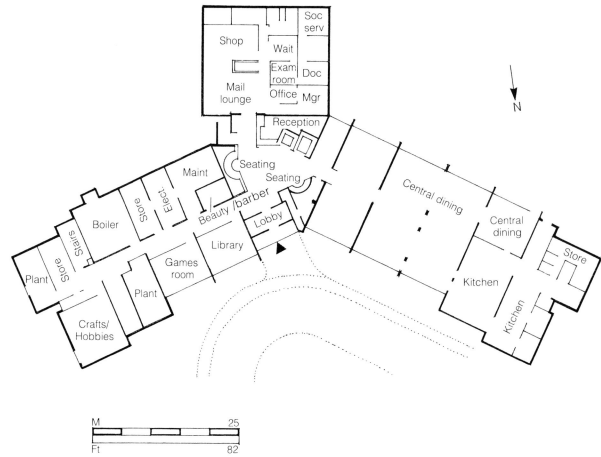

Facilities for the disabled
Apart from the specially-equipped apartments, all circulation area and doorset widths are designed to mobility standards, enabling all flats to be fitted out for disabled users.

Heating
Warm air perimeter heating from central boiler plant. Hot water also provided from central boiler.

Communal facilities
Crafts/hobby room.
Games room.
Library.
Beauty and barber shop.
Dining room.
Small general store.
Mail room/lounge.
Laundry.

Warden accommodation
No resident warden but 24 hour on-site attendance by house manager. Reception point at entrance is also manned 24 hours and the manager's office adjoins it.

Special facilities
In addition to the communal areas, Golda Meir House also has a small medical facility which includes a doctor's office and examination room, with associated waiting area. There is also a social service office within this suite, to deal with any resident's benefit problems. The reception counter by the main manager's office serves a similar function to a hotel reception, acting as a social centre where residents will stop to talk informally with the manager. The sitting area nearby is a favourite vantage point for observing the activities of the reception desk.

Comments
With consultant input from Dr S. Howell of MIT, a major planning aim was to avoid the problem of disorientation within the building. The design team included in the scheme an atrium space over the reception area: this reinforces the reception area as a focal point to the building, with the atrium providing an easily distinguishable landmark on each floor to assist in a person's orientation inside the building. The communal facilities are arranged on a 'street' off the reception

Typical floor plan.

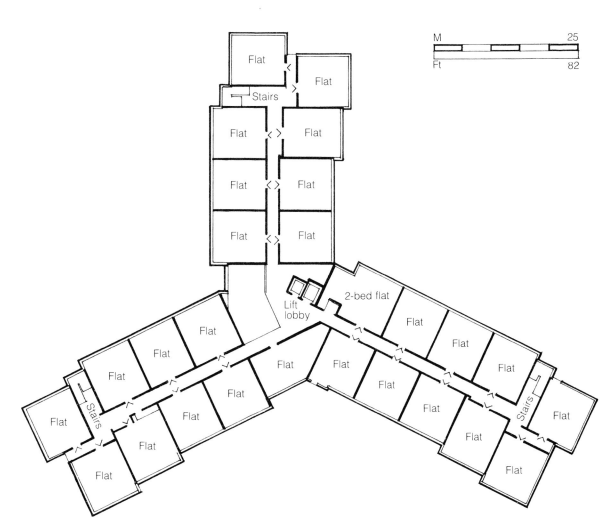

Layout of medical facility. Medical practitioners will visit the building on a regular basis and hold surgeries for residents.

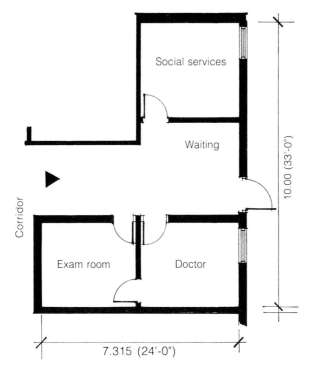

Layout of typical dwelling.

area on the ground floor. This is a deliberate attempt to introduce normal life patterns into the sheltered environment. For example, the beauty parlour, instead of being located at the end of a corridor on a second or third floor, is given a shop front and functions very much as a shop.

Bellair House

Havant, Hampshire, UK.
Completed 1986.
For: Wimpey Homes Holding Ltd.
Architects: Architects Department, Wimpey
Homes Holding Ltd.
HTA category: 3

Havant is a small and predominantly residential
area in the south of England. The development is
sited off a main road to the High Street. Because
of the nearby Havant bypass, the road is relatively quiet, and has only local traffic. Bellair
House is named after the original house which
stood on the site; as part of this development the
200 year old house was renovated and incorporated into the overall design.

Funding
Privately financed by Wimpey Homes Holding
Ltd. Flats are offered for sale on long leases.

Number and type of dwellings
26 two-person twin-bedded flats (type A).
22 two-person flats with one double bedroom
(type B).

Area of typical dwellings
Type A flat 42m² (451 sq ft)
Type B flat 38m² (409 sq ft)

Management
Hampshire Voluntary Housing Society (a
specialist management association).

Number of storeys
Ground plus two storeys.

Location/access
Bellair House is situated almost adjacent to
Havant town centre. Local facilities include
chemists, supermarkets and the local post office
is only 30 yards from the development. There is
also a small bowling green immediately opposite

*Site layout. The
original Bellair
House was reno-
vated and incor-
porated into the
development and
forms the focal
point of the
scheme.*

*A Resident Man-
ager's flat/office
(part of original
Bellair House)
B Communal
lounge
C Refuse*

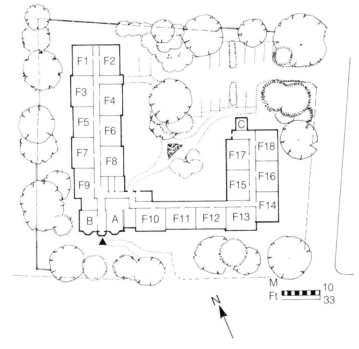

M ▬▬▬▬ 10
Ft ▬▬▬▬ 33

N

Typical flat Type A.

the site. Vehicle access is via the rear entrance from Bellair Road, and there are approximately 20 off-street parking spaces.

Facilities for the disabled
All doors are wide enough for wheelchair access. Bathrooms have assist-rails and could be adapted to mobility standards. There is one lift which connects all floors.

Heating and hot water
Independent electrical storage heating to each flat with individual immersion-heated hot water storage tank.

Communal facilities
Communal lounge
Laundry.
Guest flat.

Warden accommodation
One resident manager's flat.

Comments
Bellair House provides sheltered accommodation across the range of younger elderly (starting at 55 years) and should be capable of answering the needs of older elderly residents with some disabilities. It is typical of many of the private sheltered housing schemes for sale in the United Kingdom that have been built during the past three to four years.

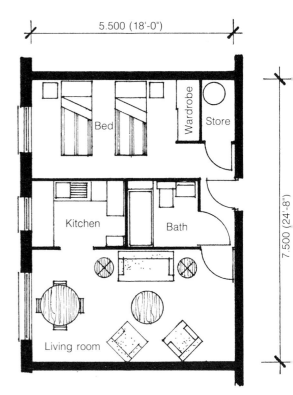

View to main entrance with the original Bellair House on left.

Living room to typical flat with kitchen access to the left.

Interior of kitchen.

Interior of bathroom.

Bedroom of show flat, very much reflecting the marketing image of traditional settings that the developer aims to project.

Though the kitchen and bathroom are not to full mobility standards, small details like easy-grip lever taps have been included.

The local post office and shopping facilities are almost next door to the development.

Courtyard area to Phase Two.

Walpole Court

Puddletown, Dorset, UK.
Completed 1984/1986.
For: The English Courtyard Association.
Architects: Sidell Gibson Partnership.
HTA category: 3

Walpole Court is situated in a secluded site in the
village of Puddletown. The site, however, is near
the village square and the meadows of the Piddle
Valley. The scheme was developed in two
phases. Phase One, completed in 1984, involved
the conversion of existing stables and cottages
dating back to the nineteenth century. Phase Two

Part of Phase One development formed by the conversion of nineteenth-century stables and cottages.

completed a year later, consists of a new-build
courtyard echoing the scale of the existing nineteenth century building.

Funding
Privately financed by Geometer Developments
Ltd: cottages and flats are offered for sale on long
leases.

Number and type of dwellings
Phase One
2 two-bedroom houses.
2 three-bedroom houses.
4 two-bedroom flats.
1 two-bedroom cottage (new-build).

Existing cottages as converted in Phase One of the development. Photo: Steve Stephens Photography.

Site plan.

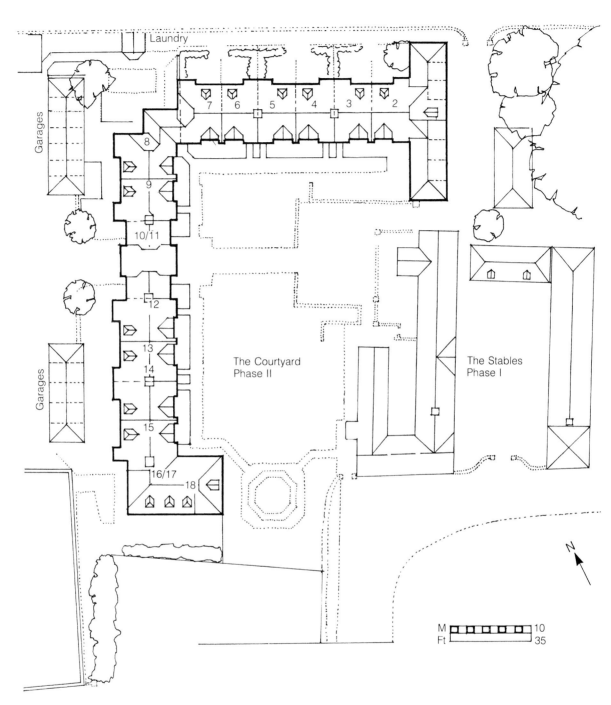

Number of storeys
Ground plus one

Location/access
The facilities of the local village are within walking
distance, for the active elderly. A local bus
service links Puddletown with the larger town of
Dorchester 5 miles away. Every cottage, and flat
has its own garage; some Phase 2 cottages have
direct access from a private patio to a garage.

Facilities for the disabled
All doors are wide enough to allow for wheelchair
access. Each bathroom is also designed to
mobility standards. In the grounds no path has a

Phase Two
9 two-bedroom cottages.
4 three-bedroom cottages.
2 two-bedroom flats.

Area of typical dwellings
Phase Two
Two-bedroom cottage 106m^2 (1142 sq ft)
Three-bedroom cottage 123m^2 (1320 sq ft)

Management
The English Courtyard Association.

Typical standard cottage.

Standard cottage as it could be adapted for future use should a resident be unable to use stairs.

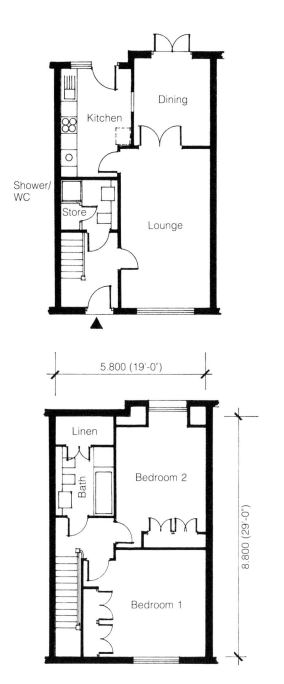

Typical standard cottage floor plan showing: Kitchen, Dining, Shower/WC, Store, Lounge

5.800 (19'-0")

Linen, Bath, Bedroom 2, Bedroom 1

8.800 (29'-0")

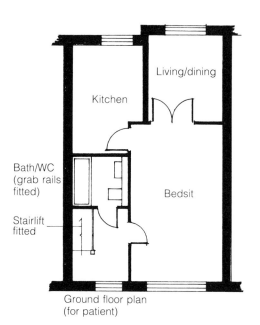

Kitchen, Living/dining, Bath/WC (grab rails fitted), Stairlift fitted, Bedsit

Ground floor plan
(for patient)

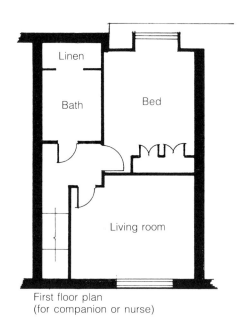

Linen, Bath, Bed, Living room

First floor plan
(for companion or nurse)

Interior of typical kitchen with access to patio outside.

Interior of typical sitting room. Note the electric log fire heater (see Chapter 7).

The laundry house.

greater slope than 1:15. Although the cottages are planned over two floors, the design provides for flexibility, in that the ground floor can only be used as a flat, allowing the upstairs suite of two rooms to be used by a relation, companion or nurse. A stair-lift could also be fitted, plus additional rail grips according to the need of each resident. For flats on the first floor a stair lift is provided.

Heating and hot water
Each cottage and flat has its own independent electric storage heating and hot water system.

Communal facilities
Guest suite.
Laundry house.

Warden accommodation
Warden's cottage.

Comments
Walpole Court provides sheltered housing at the upper end of the market for the younger and active elderly. There are no communal areas apart from a shared-use laundry and a guest suite. However, the inbuilt ability to cope with any increasing disability is interesting to note. The site layout and detail design are a deliberate effort to echo the traditional courtyard plan of the almshouses.

Rear view of cottages showing patio areas.

Main entrance with entrance canopy.

Leonard Pulham House

Halton, Buckinghamshire, UK
Completed 1982.
For: the Abbeyfield (Buckinghamshire) Society.
Architects: Salmon Speed.
HTA category: 5/6/7

The site was originally used by the Royal Air Force as a coal yard, and is bounded by trees and fields on three sides and a primary school on the fourth.

Funding
Funds raised by Abbeyfield Society mainly from private and independent sources, with no subsidy from the Housing Corporation. However, there were donations from Buckinghamshire County Council and the welfare funds of the EEC. Residents are charged a weekly fee for accommodation and support services.

Number and type of dwellings
32 single bedrooms including two bedrooms which have interconnecting doors to provide a two person bedroom.

Area of typical dwelling
14m^2.

Management
The Abbeyfield (Buckinghamshire) Society.

Number of storeys
Ground plus first.

Location/access
The site is situated in a secluded area and whilst it is not close to local shopping facilities, this is not such a critical factor for a scheme intended for frail elderly people, many of whom are building-bound. Off-street parking is provided for 10 cars.

Site plan.

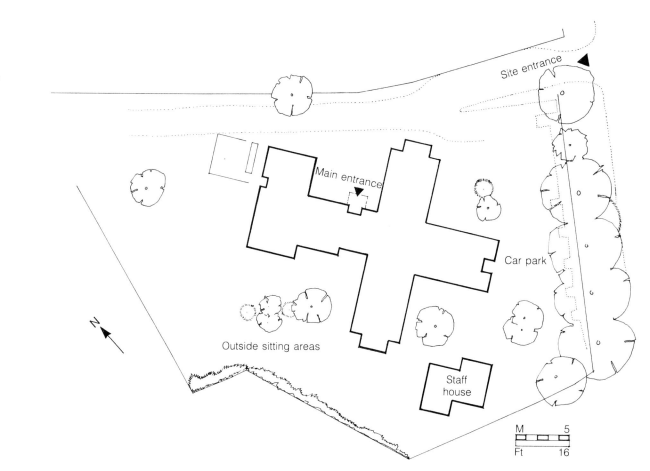

The lounge and dining rooms look out on to the development's private grounds.

Each bedroom is equipped with a fitted wardrobe and vanitory sink unit.

Ground floor plan.

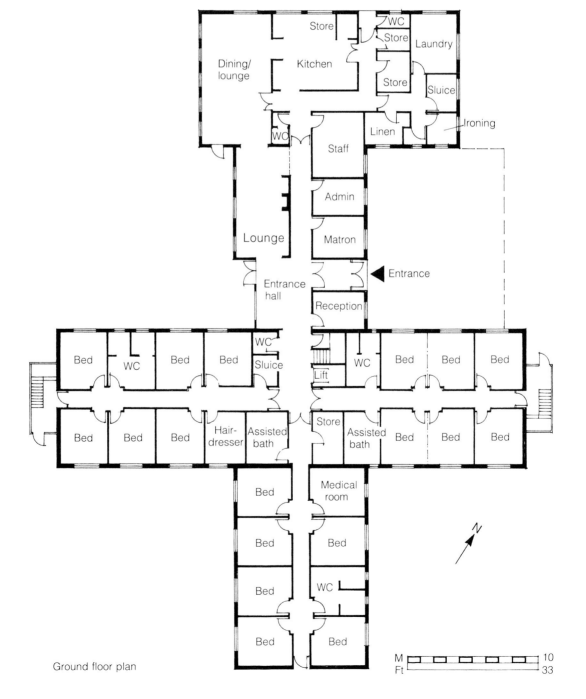

Ground floor plan

Interior of typical bedroom. Note: low window sill level ideal for sitting and looking out.

Facilities for the disabled
All rooms and communal areas are designed to cope with wheelchair users, with lift access to first floor. Each bedroom has shared access to assisted bathroom and WC.

Heating and hot water
Space heating by electric night storage heaters with conventional daytime boost. Hot water by electric point heaters.

Communal facilities
Dining room.
Lounge.

First floor plan.

N

| Bed | WC | Bed | Bed | Sluice | Lobby | Tea point | | WC | Bed | Bed | Bed |

Lift

| Bed | Bed | Bed | Bed | Assisted bath | Store | Guest | Sitting room | Bed | Bed | Bed |

M ⸻ 10
Ft ⸻ 33

Layout of typical bedroom.

Main lounge area is directly off the entrance hall.

The dining room furniture was selected to emphasise a non-institutional appearance.

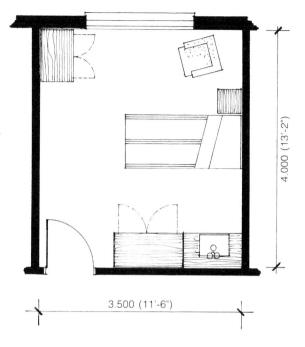

3.500 (11'-6")

4.000 (13'-2")

Hi-Lo assisted-bath as used at Leonard Pulham House, can be raised to a height comfortable for attendant. Manufactured by Mecanaids Ltd.

2 sitting rooms.
Hairdressing room.

Warden accommodation
2 four-bedroom staff houses on site for resident and deputy housekeeper.

Special facilities
As this is an extra care home, the facilities include bases for nursing care as well as services associated with central cleaning and laundry. There is a sluice room for cleaning soiled bed linen and emptying bed pans on both ground and first floors.

Comments
Leonard Pulham House is an example of the Abbeyfield Society's philosophy in caring for frail elderly people. The type of facilities offered at this scheme and the high level of nursing care are compatible with the concept of Part III and residental homes. Some residents require assistance even in minimal moving about and attendance at meals and bathing. There is 24 hour nursing cover. The bedrooms do not contain a kitchen or bathroom. Instead, bathroom and WCs are shared and grouped adjacent to the bedrooms. All meals are prepared centrally and either delivered to the rooms or served in the dining room.

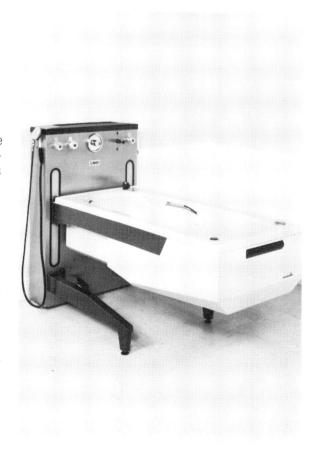

Site plan.

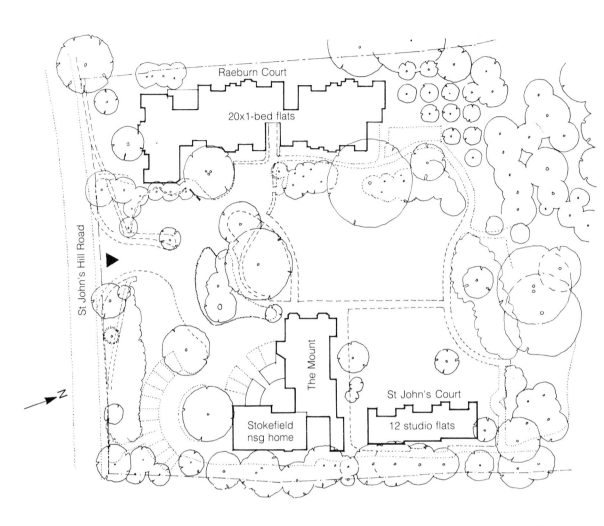

Raeburn Court

20x1-bed flats

St John's Hill Road

N

The Mount

St John's Court

12 studio flats

Stokefield nsg home

The Mount and Stokefield Nursing Home

Woking, Surrey, UK
Completed: Raeburn Court 1982; St. John's Court
1982; Stokefield Nursing Home 1986.
For: Help the Aged (Housing Division).
Architects: Hutchison Locke and Monk in
association with Geoffrey Fry (Help the Aged
Housing Division).
HTA category:
Raeburn Court   3
St John's Court   3
Stokefield Nursing Home   7

The Mount was an existing property (on the left) on the site and was donated to HTA. The new Stokefield Nursing Home is on the right.

The Mount and Stokefield Nursing Home stands
in its own grounds close to a small village centre
near the larger town of Woking in Surrey. The
immediate area consists largely of upmarket
residential properties. The development contains
on one site the following housing types and
support care:
—   The Mount: the original house on the site,
converted to provide single bedrooms with
shared WCs and containing the communal
lounges and dining room which serve the other
buildings.
—   Raeburn Court: self-contained one bedroom
flats.

—   St John's Court: self-contained studio flats.
—   Stokefield Nursing Home: single bedrooms
with shared WC facilities.
Apart from the nursing home, the accommodation is designed for the active elderly. There is
first floor accommodation with stair access only.
Stokefield Nursing Home, however, is designed
for frail elderly people who would require a high
level of nursing and personal care. Each resident
has a bedroom with wardrobe and washhand

Layout of typical flat.

5.950 (19'-6")

9.700 (32'-0")

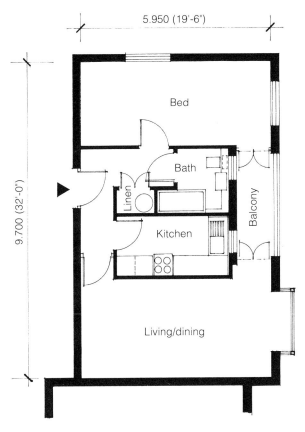

Bed

Bath

Linen

Balcony

Kitchen

Living/dining

St. John's Court taken during an HTA fund raising garden party.

The entire development is set within its own gently sloping landscaped grounds.

basin. All meals are prepared centrally, Assistance is available for those residents require help with washing or dressing and toilet functions. The Stokefield Nursing Home is not necessarily seen as a permanent home for all its residents, as it is also available for periods of convalescence or treatment following a fall or illness.

Funding
Help the Aged (HTA) is a major international charity dedicated to improving the quality of life for elderly people in need of help in the United Kingdom and overseas. They pursue this aim by raising and granting funds towards community based projects which include housing developments. The site of The Mount, including the existing house, was donated to Help the Aged. HTA then in turn funded the development of the housing accommodation, and later the nursing home, as part of its gifted housing scheme, by which a new lifestyle in a sheltered housing scheme is offered as a return to those who donate their property to the charity. The flats are offered to non-donors of HTA, who may either make a deposit which is returned in the event of their moving on, or may bequeath their estate on death. In addition, residents pay a monthly communal service charge. This method of deposit and return is currently under review at HTA – the alternative is a system by which residents' capital investment accrues and appreciates. There is also an optional claw back element whereby HTA at present claw back 5% into a care scheme. This guarantees care, which includes nursing, to all HTA residents for the rest of their lives. At the Stokefield Nursing Home, outside residents pay a weekly charge. For HTA residents or donors the weekly charge is subsidised by HTA.

Number and type of dwellings
St John's Court: 12 studio flats.
Raeburn Court: 20 one-bedroom flats.
Stokefield Nursing Home: 12 single bedrooms.

Area of typical dwellings
Studio flat 24m^2 (260 sq ft).
One-bedroom flat 56m^2 (607 sq ft).
including balcony.
Single bedroom 12m^2 (129 sq ft).

Management
Help the Aged.

Number of storeys
All two-storey.

Location/access
Local facilities are within walking distance, although this does require the negotiation of some hills. HTA, however, organise a minibus service allowing both active and frail elderly people the opportunity of visiting local facilities.

The balcony access from the living room provides an important space allowing residents to sit out without having to leave their flat.

Interior of typical living room at Raeburn Court.

Facilities for the disabled
Stokefield Nursing Home is designed to full mobility standards. However, the two-storey sheltered housing blocks are geared mainly to younger or active elderly. There is at present no lift access to the first floor as the original brief was not for wheelchair access, although plans are under way to extend Raeburn Court and incorporate a lift.

Heating and hot water
Each flat is served by its own independent gas-fired boiler for hot water and central heating. The nursing home, however, has centrally controlled gas-fired central heating and hot water.

Communal facilities
Dining room.
Lounge area.
Laundry.

Warden accommodation
A warden's flat was never planned at the Mount. However, a warden does now live in one of the sheltered housing flats. Future policy of HTA will be to provide a warden station only, which would maintain 24 hour cover by wardens who work in shifts rather than occupy a warden's flat.

Comments
The mixing of different categories of housing types on one site provides the Mount with an extended and flexible profile of care from active HTA category 3 through to frail elderly HTA category 7. The inbuilt flexibility of such a development holds important benefits for both user and developer. For the user resident there is the safeguard that the inevitable process of ageing will not necessarily force any move to a new location. This was the primary objective behind the development: to provide residents with the support and life-long care from Help the Aged within one location. Only severe illness requiring hospitalization or severe mental infirmity would necessitate a move from the site.

For the developer, he can look to a far wider range in the market. The Mount, therefore, stands as one of the first life care type developments in the United Kingdom – a type which will no doubt become more common in the years ahead.

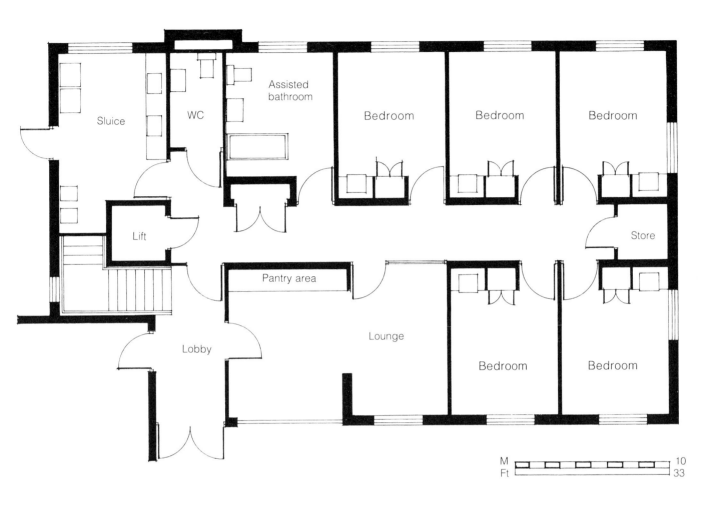

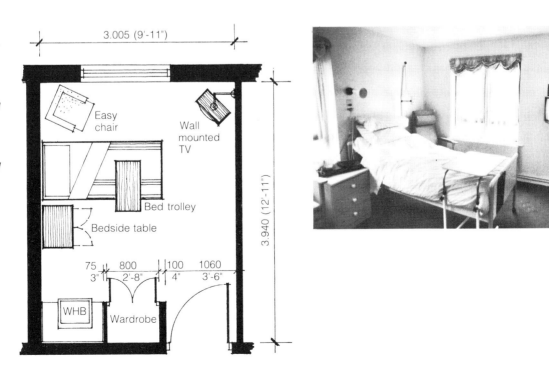

Typical floor plan for Stokefield Nursing Home.

Layout of typical bed area in Stokefield Nursing Home.

Interior of typical bed area at Stokefield Nursing Home.

The 50 self-contained villas are situated on the perimeter of the site off an access road. For entrance, see p. 75. Photos Jim Schafer.

The apartments.

Waverly Heights

Gladwyne, Pennsylvania, USA
Completed 1986.
For: Gladwyne Waverly Associates/Berwind
Realty Services Inc.
Architects: Sullivan Arfaa PC/Sullivan Associates.
Interior design: MPIB Merlino.
HTA category: 2/3/4/5/6/7

Waverly Heights is set in 53 acres of woods, gardens and open land in Gladwyne, Lower Merion, north of Philadelphia. It is primarily an upper-income residential area with low rise individual houses and small apartment buildings.

Funding
Privately financed with Berwind Realty Services Inc. Residents purchase rights to occupy their unit and pay a service charge to cover at least one meal a day, weekly maid service, towel and bed service and medical care as required.

Number and type of dwellings
50 self-contained villas which are situated on the perimeter of the site off an access road.
163 one and two-bedroom apartments.
37 nursing and personal care rooms.

Area of typical dwelling
Two-bedroom villa 130m²–147m² (1398 to 1578 sq ft)
One-bedroom apartments 78m² (836 sq ft)
Two-bedroom apartment 112m² (1208 sq ft)

Site plan of Waverly Heights.

Key
1 Gatehouse
2 Loop road
3 Villas
4 Commons
5 Nursing
6 A Apartments
7 B Apartments

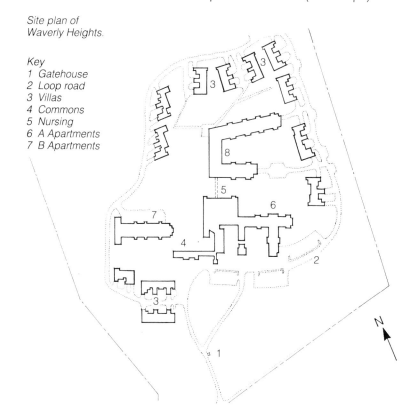

Number of storeys
Apartment buildings – ground plus two.

Location/access
The development is set back from the main entrance to the site due to the zoning constraints of the local planning code. Waverly Heights is not considered to be within walking distance of local shopping facilities. However, there is transport available to Philadelphia city centre.

Facilities for the disabled
The apartment buildings are barrier-free, allowing wheelchair users access to all units and communal facilities. For those who may experience difficulty in walking there are motorized mini-scooters for negotiating the corridors.

Heating and hot water
The 50 villas each have wood-burning fires in addition to individual heat-pump heating. All arpartments and communal areas are serviced by central heating and hot water with a central air handling unit also providing air conditioning on a chilled water loop system. An oil-fired boiler serves as a backup in case of any disruption to the gas supply.

charge. All rooms in the medical centre are single bedrooms with en-suite WC and shower. The medical centre cares for short-stay residents recovering from surgery or transient illness as well as those requiring long-term nursing care and medical supervision. Adjacent to the medical centre is an assisted living unit which can accommodate those who cannot function independently but do not need continuous medical or nursing supervision. Here residents will have bedroom and living room accommodation which they may furnish themselves. Assistance is then available with bathing, dressing and medication as necessary to maintain as far as possible the resident's sense of independence but within a personal care environment. The decision to move a resident from the villas or apartments into the medical centre or assisted living unit can only be made with the full consent of the resident, their family and medical, social and management personnel.

Comments
Waverly Heights has been developed as a comprehensive total service life care community. Although geared very much towards the upper scale of the market, it does respond to the need for such a facility in this area. The life care concept of a home for life is interpreted in terms of four quite different living arrangements, apparently to reflect the state of health and needs of a resident throughout the ageing process from the admission age of 60 years.

The villas on the perimeter of the site are for

Dining area; the management makes a point of encouraging non-residents to use the facilities as guests. The room has been carefully designed to create the atmosphere of a welcoming restaurant rather than that of a dining hall (interior design: MPIB Merlino). This encourages links with the wider community. Both lunch and dinner are available to residents: all, however, must eat at least one meal in the dining room each day. Apartment buildings are linked to all common facilities by covered walkways. Photos Jim Schafer.

Communal facilities
Dining room.
Private dining room.
Hairdressing shop.
Coffee shop.
Lounge spaces.
Bar/lounge.
Auditorium.
Indoor swimming pool and jacuzzi.
Branch bank.
Fitness and exercise gym.
Outdoor putting greens.
Library.
Card and game room.
Arts and crafts room.
Gift shop.

Warden accommodation
No 'live-in' accommodation on the site, but personal, medical and management services operate on a 24 hour basis.

Special facilities
As part of the life care concept there are facilities for licensed skilled nursing and unlimited medical care for residents aged 60 and over. This is part of the package included in the standard service

Plan of two-bed and three-bed apartments.

The heated indoor swimming pool.

any resident who can lead a totally independent life. The choice of a villa or apartment in the main block is left to the personal taste of the prospective resident. The apartment block does offer a more sheltered environment with barrier-free access to all communal facilities.

As and when an illness or accident occurs, time may be spent as an out-patient or short-term patients at the medical centre. If a resident becomes unable to function alone in an independent residential setting, the assisted living unit can provide personal care and support. Finally, when a resident is in need of continuous nursing and medical supervision, the medical facility is then available. The rationale for separate facilities for those in need of personal or nursing care is related to the licensing standards of the local health codes which set out minimum nurse supervision for bed areas.

As a reflection of market demand, plans are under way for an extension of Waverly's nursing care facilities.

Apartment kitchens have dishwashers and waste disposers, and are fitted for washing machines and tumble driers. While recognised as generous today, this should be considered as a pointer to the common expectations of future generations.

Plan of a typical villa.

Nurse's station for the medical nursing center.

The auditorium used for concerts, meetings and social gatherings.

Master bedroom

Living room

Walk-in wardrb

Bath

Dining room

Utility

Walk-in wardb

Bath

Kitchen

Hall

Bedroom

Breakfast

Garage

M ⊢━━━━━━━━┤ 5
Ft   16'-6"

Balcony

Study

Bedroom

Living/dining

Wardrobes

Wardrobe

Bath

WC

Kitchen

M ⊢━━┤ 2
Ft   6'-7"

Site plan.

1 *Communal facilities*
2 *Apartments*
3 *Skilled and personal care facility*
4 *Admin. block*

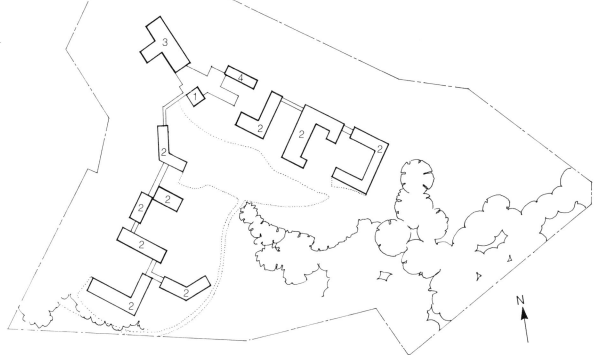

The Quadrangle

Haverford, Pennsylvania, USA
Completion: 1987–88.
For: Life Care Communities Marriott Corporation.
Architects: Wallace Roberts and Todd.
HTA category: 2/3/4/5/6/7

The Quadrangle, like Waverly Heights, is an example of the continuing interest in and investment into life care projects in the United States, and is an indication of design trends, in terms of its scale and the sophistication of facilities. The site is near Haverford College in a middle to upper-income residential area.

Funding
Privately funded via the Marriott Corporation.

Number and type of dwellings
303 one-bedroom and two-bedroom apartments.
36 secondary personal care bedrooms for assisted living.
84 primary nursing care bedrooms for skilled nursing care for frail elderly.

Area of typical dwellings (approximate only)
One-bedroom unit 74m^2 (803 sq ft).
One-bedroom unit with den 100m^2 (1077 sq ft).
Two-bedroom unit 100m^2 (1077 sq ft).
Two-bedroom unit (large) 125m^2 (1350 sq ft).

Management
Marriott Corporation.

Number of storeys
Ground plus two.

Facilities for the disabled
All circulation and communal facilities designed to mobility standards. All the apartments are joined by enclosed and covered barrier-free walkways. Apartments may be adapted for wheelchair use.

Communal facilities
Auditorium.
Library/meeting room.
Swimming pool/jacuzzi.
Coffee shop.
General store/gift shop.
Crafts and hobbies room.
Dining room.
Branch bank.
Lounge area.
Beauty shop.

Special facilities
All of the living units at the Quadrangle are linked to the communal facilities by enclosed walkways to enable easy access during inclement weather or where a resident may feel unable to venture outside. Architect Gil Rosenthal and his team at WRT Architects designed this scheme as an opportunity for residents to maintain an independent lifestyle, but within an essentially supportive community. The planning concept was to provide three levels of care:
1 Fully independent living

Model showing apartment blocks in foreground with the communal facilities building landmarked by the Bell Tower.

This would be in a self-contained one- or two-bedroom apartments. There are no bed-sitting areas ('efficiencies') at the Quadrangle, as the market demand was found to be too low to justify their inclusion.

2 Personal care

Where a resident is unable to dress without assistance or prepare their own food or to wash themselves because of physical or mental frailty and therefore needs some support to maintain a level of independence, single bedrooms are provided, each with their own bath, WC and shower, but without a kitchen. The resident will take meals in the personal care communal dining room, or may elect to dine in the skilled care dining room.

3 Skilled care

This would service the needs of the very frail elderly resident, whose state of health necessitates 24-hour nursing care. Here the resident may well be incontinent and unable to get in or out of bed or feed themselves. The resident may also require day to day medication. The facilities will be similar to those of personal care, except that only an en-suite WC is provided, and no shower. Adjacent to the skilled care facility, clinic spaces and physiotherapy facilities are provided for

Layout of the communal facility building.

1 Entrance
  quadrangle
2 Painting
  studios
3 Administration
4 Reception
5 Bank
6 Gift shop
7 Coats and
  bathrooms
8 Library
9 Lounge
10 Auditorium
11 Dining
12 Kitchen
13 Coffee shop

← To personal care units

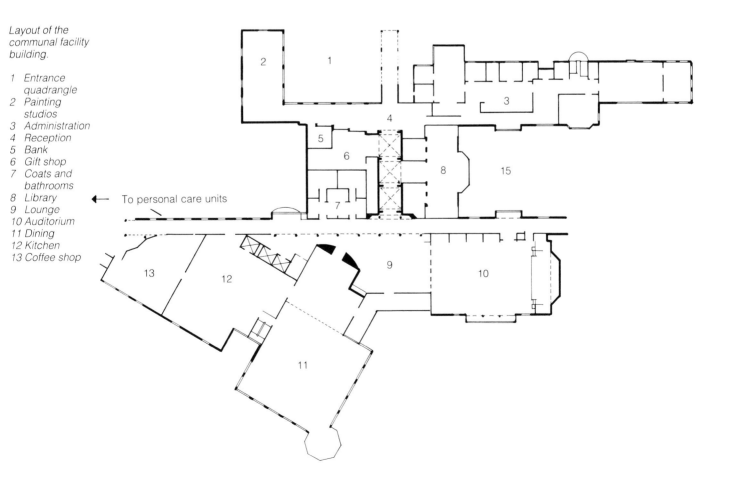

Plan of one-bedroom unit.

Plan of two-bedroom unit.

Plan of large two-bedroom unit.

M [scale bar] 6.400
Ft [scale bar] 21

2-bedroom unit (with study)

2-bedroom unit

Large 2-bedroom unit, type A

Layout of the skilled nursing facility.

32 Swimming pool
33 Physical therapy
34 Jacuzzi
35 Sun terrace
36 Residents' entrance
37 Clinic waiting
38 Clinic offices
39 Skilled care dining
40 Skilled care
41 Nurses' station
42 Bedroom (typical)

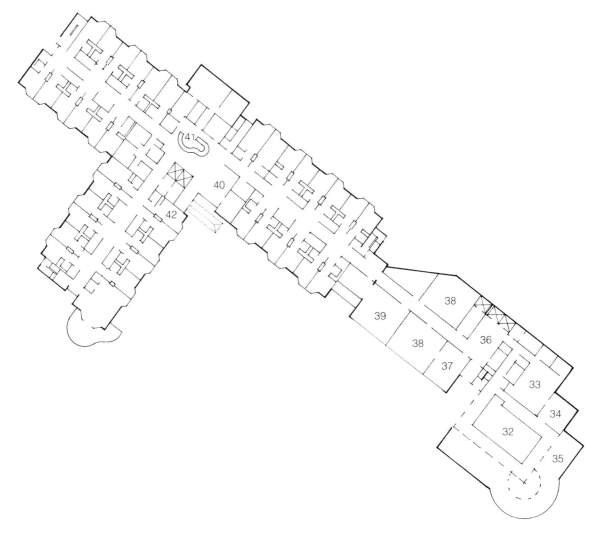

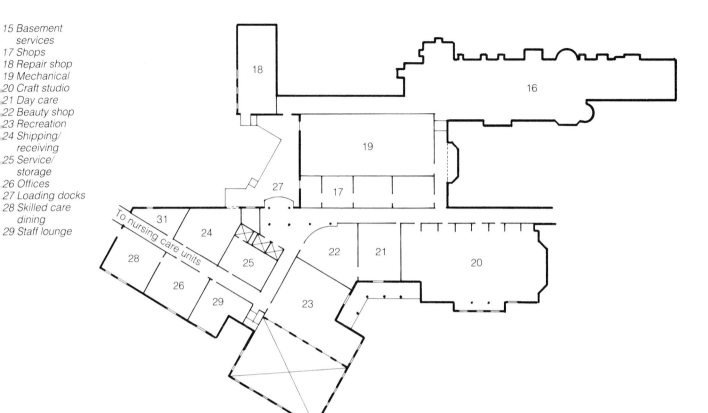

residents who may need medical attention or treatment as out-patients.

Comments
The Quadrangle very much reflects the trend in life care provision: that is, to increase the service input and communal facilities. Rather than disperse the communal areas around the campus, the concept has been to centralise them, so as to help reinforce the sense of community and to encourage residents to share the activities of their daily lives. The facilities are therefore housed in the building which is also designed to act as a central focus to the whole community.
   The design concept is to combine the college campus and a small village. Gilbert Rosenthal

As with Waverly Heights, the level of care and support is managed in different types of living units, which residents will pass through according to their temporary or permanent state of health and frailty.

Activity-based Design Criteria

Key dimensions for wheelchair user. This chapter describes the main activities of elderly people, and the associated design criteria relevant for housing elderly people. The aim is to present the activities from a user's point of view, so that the designer will understand the rationale behind certain design criteria. It is assumed that the designer or developer will already be familiar with the widely-available data on access standards for disabled or wheelchair users, though this information is summarised on pages 67–69, and references are given to the various source publications listed in the bibliography.

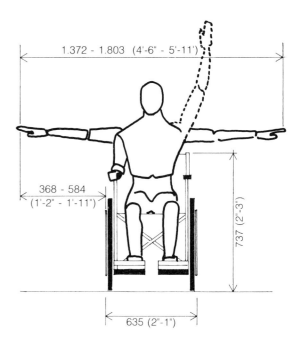

1.372 - 1.803 (4'-6" - 5'-11')

368 - 584 (1'-2" - 1'-11")

737 (2'-3")

635 (2"-1")

Key dimensions to minimum clearance for two persons in circulation areas.

Key dimensions to minimum clearance for one person in circulation areas.

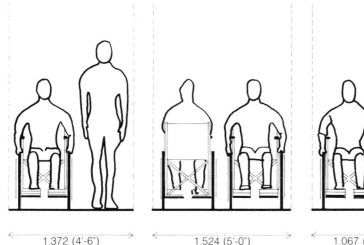
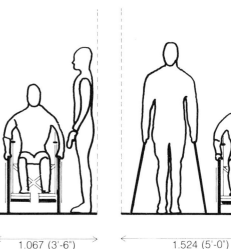

1.372 (4'-6")   1.524 (5'-0")   1.067 (3'-6")   1.524 (5'-0")

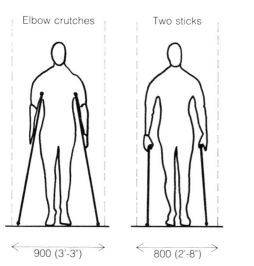

Elbow crutches   Two sticks

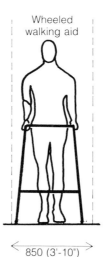

Wheeled walking aid

900 (3'-3")   800 (2'-8")   850 (3'-10")

Checklist of Key Dimensional Data

Activity	Planning allowance	Text reference (page)
Site location	200m (650 ft) to regular bus service. 600m (2000 ft) to post office, chemist/drug store.	
Entering the building	Ramp access 1:20 preferred. Maximum gradient 1:12. Distance from main entrance door to elevators to be kept between 9m (30 ft) and 24m. (80 ft) Entrance door *minimum* clear opening width 813mm (2 ft 8 in).	
Circulation areas	Corridors: Minimum (preferred) length of any corridor used by residents 30m (100 ft). A variation in corridor width between 1200mm (4 ft) and 1800mm (6ft) with increased width occurring at node points. Rough cast fairfaced brick work to be avoided up to 1524mm (5 ft). Handrails to be fixed to both sides of corridor at a height of 900mm (3 ft). Doors in circulation areas minimum clear opening width 813mm (2 ft 8 in). Lifts: Minimum two lifts to be considered in the event of one lift failing. Lift size preferred at 1100mm × 1500mm (3 ft 7 in × 4 ft) plus extension to total length of 2200mm (7ft 3in) Stairs Preferred width 1m (3 ft 4 in). Maximum pitch 35°. Preferred tread 280mm (11¼ in). Preferred riser 175mm (7 in).	
Communal facilities	Lounge areas: 3.6m² (39 sq ft) per resident (aggregate). Secondary sitting spaces to be clustered around main lounge areas or in association with family groups for 4–10 people. Allow 2.2m² (24 sq ft) per anticipated resident to use space. Dining areas 2.6m² (28 sq ft) per resident (to be increased if dining areas include for non-resident attendants).	

	Post room Minimum 0.28m² (3 sq ft) per resident. Laundry If used by residents, two 3.5kg (8 lb) washing machines and two 4.5kg (9 lb) tumble dryers per 30 dwellings. If centralised on-site staff operated facility 0.8m² (8 sq ft) per dwelling. Hairdressing/beauty parlour: 14m² (150 sq ft) should be sufficient for up to 100 residents. To be located as shop-front facility on main circulation route at ground floor.	
Shared kitchen	10m² (107 sq ft) per family group of 10 bed sitting rooms.	
Shared use facility	Assisted bathroom One assisted bath per 25 residents including a minimum of one per floor. Typical area 11m² (120 sq ft) Short stay accommodation One room at 12m² (40 sq ft) per 30 residents.	

Dwellings

Dwelling type	Metres square	Feet square
Single bed unit	14–24	150–260
Bed-sit (efficiency)	33–42	350–450
One-bedroom apartment	33–60	350–650
Two-bedroom apartment	60–93	650–1000
Three-bedroom apartment	67–260	720–2800

	Note: the actual size of dwelling units will vary according to the anticipated lifestyle and market range of potential residents. Trends in both the United States and in the United Kingdom indicate a high demand for improved space standards, particularly in the private sector. Internal doors to dwellings: minimum clear opening width 775mm (2 ft 6½ in)	
Areas used by staff	Warden's flat (if on-site accommodation is required). 70m² 753 sq ft Consulting room/Doctor's office 11m² 120 sq ft Nurse base/office 11m² 120 sq ft Clean utility 6m² 65 sq ft Dirty utility (At least one per floor) 6m² 65 sq ft	

ESTIMATED DIMENSIONS OF BODY REACH AND CHARACTERISTICS OF THE BRITISH POPULATION FOR ELDERLY WOMEN AGED 60 TO 90 YEARS.

Because in nearly all situations to which the architect applies anthropometric data, users will be clothed, the data in this table includes allowances for clothing and shoes. The allowances for footwear are 31mm (1¼in) for elderly women. The allowances for clothing affecting most of the dimensions from item 6 on, range according to circumstances from 3mm (⅛ in) to 20mm (¾ in). For areas in which clothes are not worn, as in bathrooms and shower rooms, appropriate deductions should be made. Anthropometric data in this table is from Tutt, P. and Adler, D. *New Metric Handbook*, Architectural Press, 1981.

Key dimension		Elderly women aged 60 to 90 Percentiles			Examples of applications to design problems
		5th	50th	95th	
Standing					
1 Stature	mm	1454	1558	1662	
	in	57	62½	65½	
2 Eye height	mm	1338	1441	1544	50th: Height of visual devices, view panels, notices, etc.
	in	52½	57	61	
3 Shoulder height	mm	1195	1288	1375	5th: Height for maximum forward reach.
	in	47	48½	54	
4 Hand (knuckle) height	mm	653	732	800	95th Maximum height of grasp points for lifting.
	in	25½	29	31	
5 Reach upwards	mm	1710	1852	1994	5th: Maximum height of controls – subtract 40mm to allow for full grasp.
	in	67½	73	78¼	
Sitting					
6 Height above seat level	mm	739	798	857	95th Maximum seat to roof clearance; allow for headgear (men 75mm, women 100mm) in appropriate situations.
	in	29	80	34	
7 Eye height above seat level	mm	621	684	740	50th Height of visual devices above seat level.
	in	24½	27	29	
8 Shoulder height above seat level	mm	479	529	579	5th: Height above seat level for maximum forward reach.
	in	19	21	23	
9 Lumbar height		—	—	—	50th: Height of table above seat.
10 Elbow above seat level	mm	143	193	243	50th: Height above seat or armrests or desk tops.
	in	5½	7½	9½	
11 Thigh clearance	mm	93	131	169	95th: Space under tables.
	in	3½	5	6½	
12 Top of knee, height above floor	mm	460	510	545	95th: Clearance under table above floor or footrest.
	in	18	20	21	
13 Underside thigh, height above floor	mm	366	404	442	50th: Height of seat above floor or footrest.
	in	14½	16	17½	
14 Front of abdomen to front of knees, distance		—	—	—	95th: Maximum forward clearance at thigh level from front of body or from obstruction, e.g. desk top.
15 Rear of buttocks to back of calf, distance	mm	424	470	516	5th: Length of seat surface from backrest to front edge.
	in	16½	18½	20	
16 Rear of buttocks of front of knees, distance	mm	520	579	638	95th Minimum forward clearance from seat back at height for highest seating posture.
	in	20½	23	25	
17 Extended leg	mm	890	967	1025	5th (less than): Maximum distance of foot controls, footrest etc. from seat back.
	in	35	38	40	

Key dimension		Elderly women aged 60 to 90 Percentiles			Examples of applications to design problems
		5th	50th	95th	
18 Seat width	mm	321	388	455	95th: Width of seats, minimum distance between armrests.
	in	12½	15	18	
Sitting and standing 19 Forward reach	mm	665	736	807	5th: Maximum comfortable forward reach at shoulder level.
	in	26	29	34	
20 Sideways		—	—	—	5th: Limits of lateral finger tip reach; subtract 130mm to allow for full grasp.
21 Width over elbows		—	—	—	95th: Lateral clearance in work space.
22 Shoulder width	mm	381	431	481	95th: Minimum lateral clearance in work space above waist.
	in	15	17	19	

For other key dimensions diagrams see also the following pages:

The various sections of this chapter also contain generic plans, block plans, and comparative plan types.

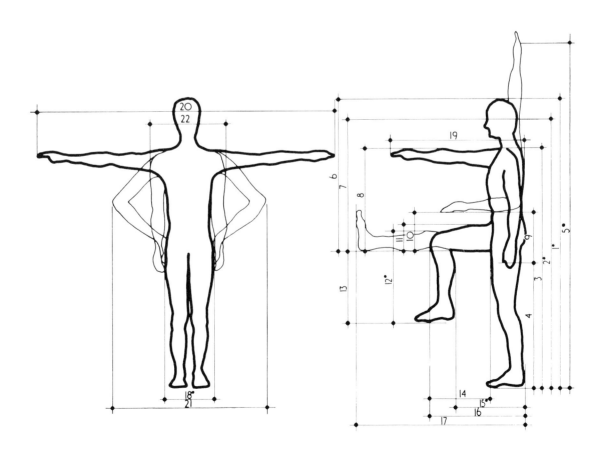

The journey to local facilities is a vital link in maintaining the ability to experience the outside world. But the degree to which it can be enjoyed, especially by the less active, will depend upon a whole range of small but important factors.

A major criterion of a site's suitability will be its nearness to local shopping and transport facilities.

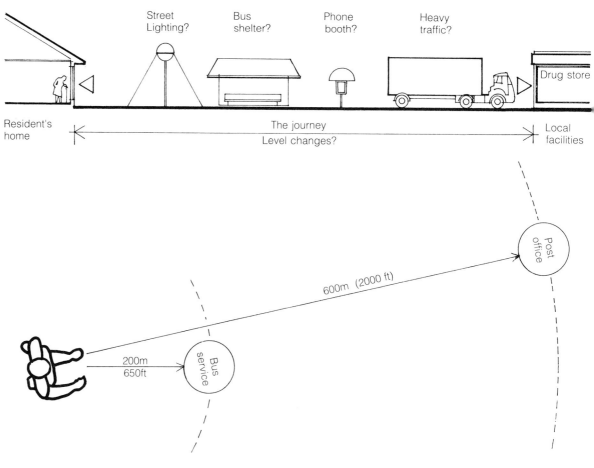

Street Lighting? Bus shelter? Phone booth? Heavy traffic? Drug store

Resident's home | The journey / Level changes? | Local facilities

Post office

600m (2000 ft)

200m 650ft

Bus service

Site Selection

A critical factor in the development of any housing project for elderly people will be the quality of the site selected. Site selection should ideally consider at once the feasibility of a project from the financial, geographical, technical, planning and design viewpoints.

Financial feasibility
The architect's first task will invariably be to appraise the site that a funding agency or developer has already identified.

Some developers, particularly public authorities, may carry out their own feasibility study in-house prior to appointing an architect. Others, however, will rely far more on an architect on a project-to-project basis to give them a first clue. Michael Foster

Each developer will tend to have his own priorities within any set of criteria for site selection. The following information should therefore be established at a preliminary stage by both the architect and developer:
1 What were the criteria for the developer in first considering the site as a possibility?
2 Has any preliminary research been carried out as to what type of demand exists for housing

elderly people in the area? If so, is it compatible with the type of market that is aimed at?
3 What number and type of units does the developer anticipate accommodating on the site?

Beyond carrying out a survey to determine how well the site is located, the first item of work we would carry out is to determine how many units will fit onto the site. This can be carried out as a relatively quick exercise to determine whether x number of units plus x number of car parking spaces might fit on the site, so that the developer can decide whether to pursue the site any further. John Eatwell.

4 Has the developer investigated whether there are likely to be any similar proposals in the area?

We always recommend that a thorough study be done in terms of marketing to determine whether there is a sufficient constituency to support such a facility. This is because a site may answer all the requirements of a superb location but fail from the standpoint that there will be no market there. One would also have to consider the type of life-style of the residents that your market area is going to deal with. You have, therefore, to search out the nature of those kind of facilities people from that particular background would anticipate being available. Joe Jordan

Site location

When you are still active, then you can get into your car and drive to the shops. As you become less active, the ability to drive and the desirability of driving becomes less, so you need to be able to walk to the shops. Peter Phippen

The importance of the site being within walking distance of local shopping facilities is a key site selection factor. The term walking distance is of course a highly subjective one. However, it is here taken to mean a distance that a person aged 60 years plus might reasonably be expected to walk, in both directions, without assistance.

In particular, the availability of the following services within such a distance would be seen as a distinct advantage by both the developer and potential resident:
Post office (for pensions/benefits)
Food shops
Doctor's and dentist's surgeries
Chemist
Branch bank
Library
Park
Church
Public house
Day centre

Because residents may also tend to rely on public transport, the proximity of public transport routes should also be carefully considered. Walking distance should, however, not be measured by linear distance alone, but also in terms of any levels that may have to be negotiated. The negotiation of a steep climb or descent to local facilities will deter many residents from venturing out at all.

The exact route which has to be taken to the local facilities should therefore be examined in detail. For example, are there any major roads to cross? If so, is there a pedestrian crossing? Is the route well lit at night? Is the route subject to any security problems? If there is a slope, is it downhill for the return journey? What is the condition of the pavements? Is the route subject to heavy traffic? Is there a bench on the way to rest on, or a bus shelter in case of a sudden rainstorm? And is there a telephone box in case of an emergency?

Age Concern recommends that a regular and frequent bus service should be situated within 200 metres (650 ft) and a facility such as a post office and chemist should, where possible, be available within 600 metres (2,000 ft). It has been suggested that to overcome such potential hazards, many such facilities could be provided within the development. However, this may be counter-productive.

It's not good enough to propose that such services or facilities could be provided on site, as people do need to get out. This is not so much to do with what people may need, it's because of the ability to maintain social contact which is so important. Peter Phippen

It isn't just the need to be near local facilities, but just as important is the quality and the richness of the experience of the walk. The opportunity to window-shop and to occasionally go into a store or café are essential factors in the criteria for site selection. This is because such factors reinforce the being a part of a larger community. Dr Sandra Howell

For the older elderly, as walking becomes more difficult, the nearness of such facilities will determine that point at which it will become too difficult to go out.

I go out every day to the shops, even if it's just to buy a newspaper. I could have it delivered but I like to dress up and put my best coat on and see what's going on. Resident (Fullwell Court, Milton Keynes, England)

Access for visitors (i.e. proximity of public transport) is also a factor to consider. This is especially important for those who have become housebound. Their quality of life will now depend upon social interaction within the site.

The character of the site and its compatibility with the immediate environment should also be considered. The move to integrate schemes more into the local fabric of the community, however, brings with it its own related problems of security. In the United States elderly people suffer a serious problem from the antagonism of malevolent teenaged children. To reduce the potential danger, many projects are opting for complete segregation from children of all ages.

The middle way is perhaps in the selection of a site that can both be near the local environment and enjoy the ability to control access, not just to the building but to the site as a whole.

Other factors

The equation of feasibility will of course also involve such more conventional methods of site appraisal as the local planning authority's view of such a development in terms of land use, and the scale of any proposal. Further factors will be the technical investigation of the soil type and the availability of public utilities.

Traditional courtyard concept of the early almshouses. This allowed for dwellings to have a double aspect, with views both into the courtyard and outside, perhaps to areas of activity.

Double loading of corridors with single aspect dwellings. If views out from the corridor are only of the courtyards this could be disorientating for some residents.

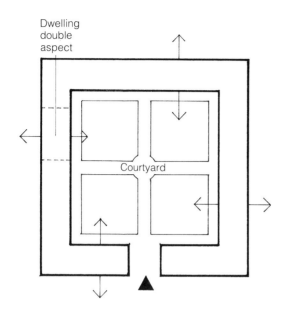

Dwelling double aspect

Courtyard

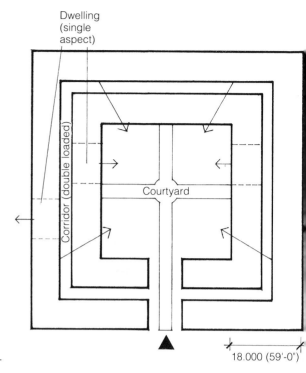

Dwelling (single aspect)

Corridor (double loaded)

Courtyard

18.000 (59'-0")

Site Planning

Ideally, all habitable rooms should enjoy a southerly aspect. However, as with any housing development, the site will to a great extent dictate the form of the layout.

Housing for the elderly perhaps draws one of its strongest site planning traditions from the courtyard plans of the early almshouses in the United Kingdom. The very notion of a courtyard implies a controlled orientation, with importance placed upon a pre-designed view out from the dwellings. The English Courtyard Association has respected this tradition and developed it as a major theme of its own sheltered housing, but uses double-aspect units having views both into the courtyard *and* outside.

Phippen Randall & Parkes's scheme for extra-sheltered housing for the United Kingdom Housing Trust at Daventry. Their design allows for a variety of views either onto the adjoining street or onto the entrance courtyard and car park.
(Illustrations by Phippen Randall & Parkes).

We looked at the type of layouts of the almshouses built during the eighteenth century and discovered the variety that could be produced from the simplest basic plan. In planning a site we think of the buildings as a horizontal block of flats. People will be buying, say, one-thirtieth of a stake in the whole scheme. Therefore they are not buying just an individual flat or cottage: it is the total environment that matters. We studied the way in which small buildings have been fitted into groups in country estates. This was the inspiration behind developing the courtyard concept.
Paul Gibson

Focussing all units on to a courtyard or one particular viewpoint of course presupposes the ability to have single-loaded circulation routes.
However, the need to maintain economic densities, in terms of the number of units to be accommodated, will invariably lead to at least a proportion of the circulation spaces being double-

he factor that emains important vill not be the mount of direct unlight but the quality of the view hat each dwelling nay enjoy; Avenue Road, London, for ondon Borough of Haringey (archiects, and illustraon: Marden and Knight).

Conceptual planing at feasibility tage should Jetermine optimum orientation for dwellings in terms of their views out as vell of as the numbers and sizes of units that can be accommodated on the site.

loaded. It is in this situation that the courtyard concept may actually be detrimental to appropriate housing for elderly people.

The courtyard can be disorientating because of its relative uniformity for the person walking along a double-loaded corridor, with the only view out from that corridor being the courtyard. This will aggravate disorientation. If all the corridors are essentially identical and are going around the courtyard in a circle, there will be nothing to tell you where you are in the building and where you are in relation to the outside.

The other disadvantage of the courtyard layout is related to a fundamental misconception that elderly people will only want passive views, and of passive places. Most gerontologists will agree that it is activity that people want to be orientated to. So, to have everything focused on a passively used and predominantly empty internal courtyard will not be conducive to creating a stimulating environment'. Dr Sandra Howell

Double-loading of corridors will therefore lead to units within the same scheme having different and opposing orientation. The factor that remains important will not be so much the direct sunlight, as the view that each dwelling may enjoy.

A view is important, not because elderly people will want to look out from where they live any more than anyone else; but rather because the amount of time that they may spend within their dwelling gives the view out of it an increased significance for them.

The orientation of building windows and seating areas is normally thought of as a function primarily of weather and sunlight. Certainly, these factors are important, but I would feel that where you are dealing with an older population they should at least be moderated by concern for what one can see. In working on the trade-offs, there may be some occasion when the ability to watch interesting activities or to have good surveillance for security purposes may be so important that something a little less desirable in terms of sunlight orientation may have to be accepted. Dr M. Powell Lawton

As people become frail, the view of something happening that is not just a view becomes more important. As physical disabilities restrict one's mobility, there can be a sense that the boundaries of one's life are closing in. For the very frail, who would be virtually house-bound, the view out from the dwelling or sitting room can become the only window onto the outside world. Peter Phippen

Although some guidance notes do advise views onto areas with plenty of activity, the possibility of enjoying a variety of viewpoints from within the scheme would seem more appropriate, and would suit individual preferences better.

Entering the Building

Activity
One's first experience of a building, either as a visitor or prospective resident, will be of the main entrance. The quality of the design and the ease with which a person may negotiate their journey into the building will certainly influence their first impression.

More importantly, the access in and out of the building, marking the boundary between the sheltered environment and the outside world, should ideally allow that boundary to be crossed easily.

Apart from those schemes designed as individual cottages in which each dwelling will have its own front door entrance, most schemes will have one main entry point from which the main circulation route will run. Everyone entering or leaving the building will therefore pass through the main entrance. This underlines the importance of this area as a main focus of activity.

I think you have to accept that there is a total difference between designing a building which basically has one entrance, and designing self-contained flats, because without the external front doors the scheme can appear institutional. Therefore, what happens on the ground floor is very important. Peter Phippen

Despite the fact that many residents may not actually leave their dwelling during the day (especially during inclement weather) there will still be a variety of people who visit the building. Apart from relatives and friends, health visitors, social workers, doctors and the like provide a steady stream of comings and goings through the main entrance. Residents waiting for a taxi or relatives will also need to congregate around this area.

People who can't go out, for example the husband who has arthritis, will go down with his wife and wait near the entrance for her to return. Peter Phippen

The area around the main entrance therefore becomes a focal point of the building.

Design criteria
— The main entrance should be clearly visible from first entering the site, to help both visitor and

Entering the building: design considerations.

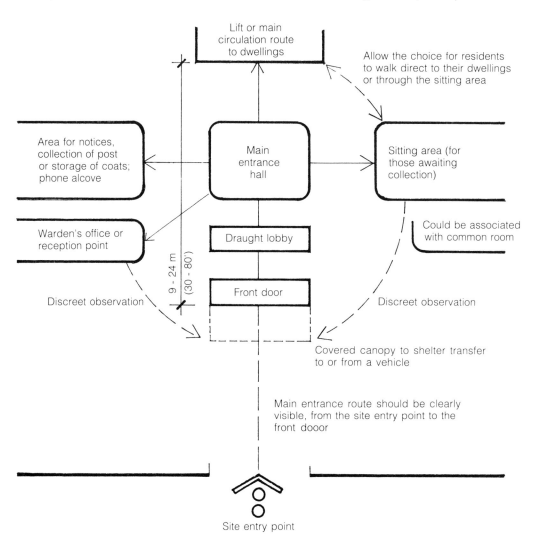

Entering the building: design considerations.

Waverly Heights: a canopy to offer shelter as people transfer in or out of vehicles will be important. Residents, especially those less ambulant, may take some time getting into or out of a vehicle (architects: Sullivan Associates for Gladwyne Waverly Associates, photo Jim Schafer).

'The front door should be a front door'. Geoffrey Salmon. A wide single-leaf door with easy grip ironmongery with an extra leaf for use when loading large items is provided at BUPA House, Milton Keynes (architects: Salmon Speed for BUPA).

The front entrance is clearly visible from the moment the site is entered at BUPA House, Milton Keynes, UK (architects: Salmon Speed for BUPA).

resident find their way into the building without confusion.

— The point of entry to the site should be easy to supervise visually, ideally from the warden's office near the main entrance, both to improve security and to make it possible to attend to anyone in difficulty immediately outside the building.

— The pedestrian route from the point of entry to the site to the main entrance should be clearly indicated and segregated from any vehicular traffic route. The route should also be well-lit.

— Whilst changes in level should be avoided, where these do occur they should be designed for wheelchair access. Ramps and gradients should preferably be 1:20, with a maximum of 1:12. However, for anyone using a walking frame a ramp can also prove difficult and sometimes a hazard. Steps should therefore be provided as well as ramps. The stairs should have both adequate size treads and not too steep a pitch: the Scottish Housing Handbook recommends a maximum pitch of 35°[1]. It will also be important to introduce a distinction in colour between the treads and the risers, and an easily gripped and visually distinguishable handrail.

— By the use of changes in colour or texture ample warning of any change in level should be clearly indicated.

— The entrance door itself should be easy to perceive and to distinguish from any other external doors and should have a minimum clear opening width of 813mm (2 ft 8 in).

— Door ironmongery should also be easily distinguished and easy to grasp (see chapter 7).

— Where possible, external doors should not be spring-loaded but easy to open.

— At the doorset, raised thresholds could prove a hazard: levels on both sides of the front door should therefore be equal.

— A canopy to offer shelter as people transfer in and out of vehicles from the main entrance will be important. Residents, especially those less ambulant, may take some time getting in or out of a vehicle.

— As with most buildings with a high through-put of people during the day, the provision of a daught lobby is desirable for reasons of security, heat loss and maintenance of floor finishes.

— Inside the building a sitting space should be provided, with a view out to the main entrance area to enable residents to watch for the arrival of visitors or a taxi. This will also provide a popular space for those residents who may merely want to observe the comings-and-goings of the building. It should be recognised, however, that there will be some residents who may not wish to feel as if they are being watched as they pass through the main entrance. The design of the waiting area should therefore allow for a discreet viewing of the main entrance rather than obvious surveillance.

A small sitting area directly off the main entrance is used by residents waiting for visitors at Golda Meir House, Newton, Massachusetts (architects: Larkin Glassman and Prager).

The common room at Mount Pleasant Lane, London, overlooks the main entrance area, providing a popular space for those residents who may just want to observe the comings-and-goings of the building (architects: Anthony Richardson and Partners).

— Because the prime purpose of most people entering the building will simply be to go to their own dwelling, the distance between the main entrance door and the lifts should be kept to a minimum. This is especially important in multi-storey developments. Howell suggests that this distance should be preferably between 9 m (30 ft) and 24 m (80 ft) in length[2]. That is, long enough to accommodate the activities associated with entering the building but without encouraging the thought that any unauthorised visitor could easily slip into the building and use the lift. The distance, however, should not be too long, for the sake of people carrying shopping bags.

Preferably there should be one entrance and that entrance itself should be as domestic as it can be. That is, trying not to have double doors but attempting to keep everything as simple and direct as possible. Immediately adjoining this area there should be a small sitting space, which in itself can be an extension of the communal lounge. Peter Phippen

— Because some residents may not always be able to leave the building, it will be important that the design allows for a sense of contact with what goes on outside the building.

I don't see any difference between designing the outside of a building and designing the inside. As soon as you step onto a site a building should begin to enclose you. This is, at best, a sequence of events where the sense of enclosure becomes more and more as you enter the building. But as you get into the building there should be a variation of inside and outside. Peter Phippen

The main entrance will also provide a central point for collecting any post or for displaying messages or notice to residents. In some schemes, mail is delivered personally to each dwelling. However, a central collection area appears to be becoming more popular with the warden/house manager or other residents who deliver mail to those unable to leave their dwelling (see chapter 6, pp. 92–93).

— Sufficient space should be allocated for notice boards. Residents may wish also to pin their own notices, so these should be at an accessible height.

— A public telephone alcove (rather than a box) would be useful for relatives of visitors calling for a taxi or to check on an appointment in case of a late arrival.

— There should also be provision for the storage of hats and coats, for visitors who may only use the communal areas. Similarly, a store off the hall should be provided for wheelchairs and walking aids.

— Methods of security control will vary according to the policy of the funding authority and any security problems of a particular area. A warden's office next to the entrance provides some protec-

tion. However, the nature of the warden's duties means that only a limited time is actually spent in the office. The use of entryphones appears to be increasing, especially in urban areas. They can malfunction, but the need to prevent unauthorised entry tends to take precedence over the disadvantages of the entryphone system.

— Most service deliveries are also best handled via the main entrance. However, where bulk deliveries are undertaken, as to the main kitchen areas, a separate service access point, locked when not in use, should be considered. As with the deliveries of post, daily delivery of milk appears to take two different forms, according to management policy; some schemes let the milkman in to deliver and to call upon each dwelling, and allow the residents themselves to be responsible for payment. In other schemes, however, milk is delivered to the main entrance and is collected from there by the resident.

Key dimensions to public telephone booth.

Raised thresholds should be avoided. Instead, thresholds with compressible Neoprene inserts are recommended.

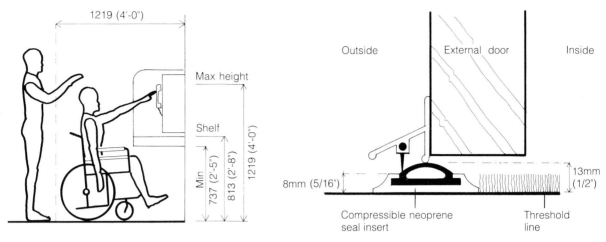

Max height

Shelf

1219 (4'-0")

Min 737 (2'-5")
813 (2'-8")
1219 (4'-0")

Outside   External door   Inside

8mm (5/16")

13mm (1/2")

Compressible neoprene seal insert

Threshold line

Key dimensions for minimum lobby widths taking into account wheelchair access.

Note: internal doors within dwellings are sometimes better reduced to a minimum of 775mm (2 ft 6½ in) to maximise usable floor space.

305 (1'-0")

Clear opening 813 (2'-8")

305 (1'-0")

Access for doors in alignment

2134 (7'-0")   305 1'-0")

813 (2'-8") Clear opening

305 (1'-0")

305 (1'-0")

Access for doors at right angles

Key dimensions to ramp access and external stairs.

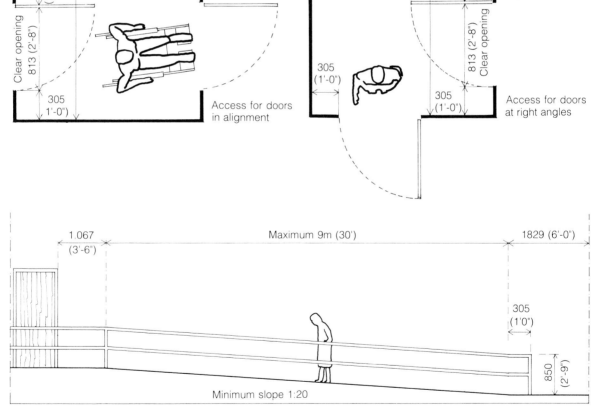

1.067 (3'-6")   Maximum 9m (30')   1829 (6'-0")

305 (1'0")

850 (2'-9")

Minimum slope 1:20

Ramp access

380 (1'-3")

140 (5½")

External stairs

At Springfield
Court, Milton
Keynes, which is a
single storey
development, top
light is used to
dramatic effect,
creating an internal
street with quarry
tile floors, planting
and seating areas
(architects: Milton
Keynes Develop-
ment Corporation).

For key dimen-
sions in circu-
lation areas, see
the beginning of
this chapter and
also p. 83.

Moving around the Building: Circulation Areas

Activity
The circulation areas perhaps more than any
other space in the building will bring into focus
the need for the designer to be aware of the implications of the mental and physical disabilities that
may occur over time to residents.

*As an architect, I have a prejudice against the
experience of corridor: very often they are ill pro-
portioned, non-stimulating and non-differentiat-
ing. Since any circulation area will become an
important part of the life of an elderly person, a
stimulating circulation environment becomes a
critical factor. Joe Jordan*

As previously discussed in chapter 3, one of the
conditions of mental frailty is confusion, which
can occur when a person becomes out of touch
with their surroundings. This can be further
aggravated by a move to a new environment. A
major design objective should therefore be to
ensure that the environment does not contribute
to confusion or disorientation, but instead allows
residents to move around the building without the
anxiety of getting lost or confused.

For residents who may have previously lived in
self-contained houses, the corridor will represent
a new experience. Sandra Howell's research in
the United States reveals that in one development
she studied, residents describe their corridors as
'like a cell block, cold and uninviting'[3].

Perception of a corridor can also change over
time, as a result of the ageing process. Sandra
Howell has described how reduced visual acuity
can lead to a long corridor of 30–60m
(100–200 ft) being perceived as a tunnel, with
approaching figures appearing distorted[4].

Apart from mental frailty, the ability to walk can
become more restricted over time, so that distances become more critical. As one resident
explained to me.

*Every day it seems to take a little longer to walk
back to my room. It must be old age. Resident,
Golda Meir House, Newton, Massachusetts.*

If circulation distances are too far, at best this will
cause an unnecessary nuisance to residents and
at worst it will contribute to restricting their abilitiy
and desire to leave their dwelling. For those
residents who may become building-bound,
especially during inclement weather, the walk
along the corridor to, say, the communal lounges
will be their only experience of getting out. This,
considered with the slower pace that many
elderly, especially the frail, will walk, stresses the
importance of paying attention to the detail
design of these areas.

*The first criterion for a corridor area must be a
rationality and clarity of circulation. At certain
stages in an elderly person's development the*

Articulating corri-
dors by introduc-
ing node points
about the entran-
ces to the
dwellings adds
variety and inter-
est. Nodes should
not be more than
5m (16 ft) apart.

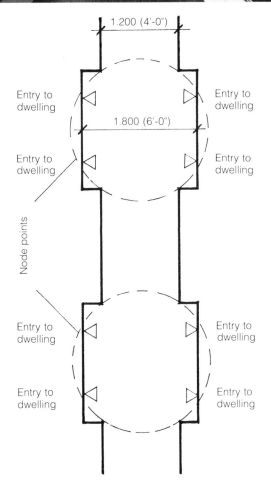

An essential feature to the circulation routes will be a handrail fixed on both sides of the corridor at a height of 900mm (3 ft).

Corridors varying in width, interest and variety at Home Life House, Bexhill-on-Sea, UK. The architect and interior designers provide a welcoming interior successfully playing down the scale of the building and colour coding each floor very much in a co-ordinating form (architects: Architects Department of Home Life Care Ltd – a subsidiary company of McCarthy and Stone – and with assistance from Fitch and Company on furnishings and colour schemes).

View out from the circulation areas will also help to orientate a person as to where they are in the building in relation to the site.

Circulation routes at The Mount, Woking UK, are punctuated with small daylit alcoves introducing a variety of lighting and texture (architects: Hutchison Locke and Monk).

Adequate provision should be planned into the circulation areas for wheelchairs to be parked when not in use.

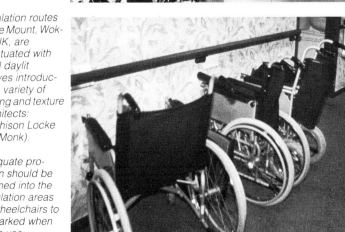

Windows arranged on the side walls (where possible) allow for daylight to enter the corridor without the problems of glare; Golda Meir House (architects: Larkin Glassman and Prager).

Notice boards cannot only serve to help personalize and add interest to the circulation areas, they can also become landmarks in the journey through the corridor. It will be important, however, to position the notice boards and any associated signage at the right height for them to can be easily read by the residents.

ability to deal with 'where am I?', 'where am I going?' and 'how do I get there?' become a significant problem; so people do need visual clues from their immediate environment to achieve that objective. Joe Jordan

The function of a circulation space is, however, not just to provide the most efficient method of connecting A to B. Rather, it should be a space that may be enjoyed in its own right.

For buildings that are not used by the same people every day (i.e. hospitals) a prime concern is the simplification of circulation routes as a strict function of getting people about the building. But we look at circulation in housing for elderly people as the spaces that people are going to get to know and experience as humane and interesting. Peter Phippen

Joe Jordan has also explained that a genuine and often missed opportunity is the attraction for residents of using the corridor as an observation point.

Particularly for frail elderly people, it is very common for residents to want to station themselves outside their room in chairs along the corridor because this is where the nurses are going back and forth. It therefore becomes something to observe. However, if the corridor width is too narrow this can seriously interfere with the operation of staff and therefore may not be permitted by management. Joe Jordan

The image that a building projects, especially upon one's first visit, perhaps as a prospective resident, will be influenced by the design of its circulation spaces. Whilst financial consideration can cause the materials specification and even the sizing of the circulation areas to be pared down, a building with even the best thought-out flat layouts and communal facilities will still appear institutional if its corridors seem utilitarian and unrelieved.

Design criteria
—   The length of any corridor used by a resident should be kept to a minimum, ideally no more than 30m (100 ft), so as not to discourage movement about the building, especially by frail elderly people.
—   The width of the corridors used by residents should also not be too narrow or too uniform in width as narrow, uniform corridors can contribute to an institutional atmosphere.
—   The more successful corridors appear to be those with a variety in their character and width. Articulating the corridor space can give meaning to the entrances of the flats themselves.

We try to create something at the entrance to a dwelling because people may wish to colonise the area outside their entrance door, so we trend to recess entrance doors, which in turn adds definition to the corridor itself. Peter Phippen

The introduction of recessed points of entry into rooms and the clustering of doors achieves a modulation through the corridor which can be reinforced with lighting to accent the points of entry. This can all significantly contribute to differentiating the corridor spaces. Joe Jordan

These recessed nodes could also perhaps be designed as discreet internal balconies, where residents may sit by their front door.
—   A variation in corridor width between 1200mm (4 ft) and 1800mm (6 ft) is therefore desirable, with the increased width occurring at nodal points, either where a view may be enjoyed or at the entrance to a flat.
Clear opening widths of doors to circulation areas should be a minimum of 813mm (2 ft 8 in).
—   The introduction of natural light into corridor spaces, although important, is not always easy. Because the most economic plans will tend to have double-loaded corridors, the opportunity to let in daylighting may only occur at the ends of corridors, or via staircases. However, as Joe Jordan has explained, the introduction of a window at the end wall of a corridor should be avoided.

A frequent problem with corridors is the installation of windows at the far end of a corridor wall, which then creates an extreme glare problem. While this is usually done to make a cheerful view, it means that in reality the glare blots your vision

Windows at the end walls of corridors should be avoided as these can create glare and distort the image of approaching figures.
Here the use of hard reflective surfaces to both the floor and walls aggravates the problem. Also, note no shelf for storing milk bottles necessitating residents bending down to retrieve them.

Good shadowless light is essential in staircases. Widths should not exceed 1 metre (3 ft 4in) with continuous handrails each side. Leonard Pulham House, Halton, Bucks, UK (architects: Salmon Speed).

out as you are approaching the window; so this has to be handled in a more subtle way. Instead, the design should look for opportunities to introduce daylight and views out through the side walls of the corridor. Joe Jordan

One of the most successful examples of the use of daylight in a circulation space is at Springfield Court, Milton Keynes, England, where a single-storey corridor is top lit.

In most cases, only side lighting from windows will be possible. However the atrium, a concept now becoming popular in some office and retail development, has yet to by fully explored in housing projects for elderly people. The advantage of the atrium is that it can transform circulation spaces into interior spaces with a vertical connection to upper levels. It is recognised that this can be a more costly solution, but its potential benefits should at least be considered.

Especially during inclement weather, the corridors should function as places where people want to walk, to make possible the casual meeting.

I like to think the corridor should be different from the inside of the flat. It's important to keep as rich and as varied an environment as possible. These are not like hotel corridors, because it should not be somewhere where you identify a person just by the number on their room. Instead, the corridor should take on some of the imagery of a street with each flat entrance having the opportunity to be a little different. Peter Phippen

— The liberal provision of clocks, notice boards and pictures, placed at eye-level, will add to the interest of the space, and help to remind residents where they are in relation to the rest of the building.

— The interior finishes of a corridor can help alleviate the institutional qualities associated with corridor design. Finishes can also help to distinguish parts of the building from each other, to break down the scale and to avoid uniformity and its the tendency to disorientate residents.

— Many schemes have adopted colour coding to distinguish each floor. This can work to a degree, although there is sometimes a conflict between the selection of a suitable colour for a particular space and the need to be able to distinguish the colours on the different floors from each other.

— Floor numbers should be clearly visible from the entrance, in this case the stair and lift lobbies of each floor. As well as the use of colour coding, considering should also be given to providing landmarks beside the lift/stair lobby, such as a small sculpture or a painting, to reinforce the identity of each floor. As one moves along the corridor, the presence of painting or prints along the wall will help personalise the space as well as, again, providing discreet landmarks.

A variation in the scale and character creating incidental sitting areas where the building turns in the main circulation route has been achieved in this scheme at Boston Court for Berwickshire District Council, Scotland (architects: Bain Swan Architects).

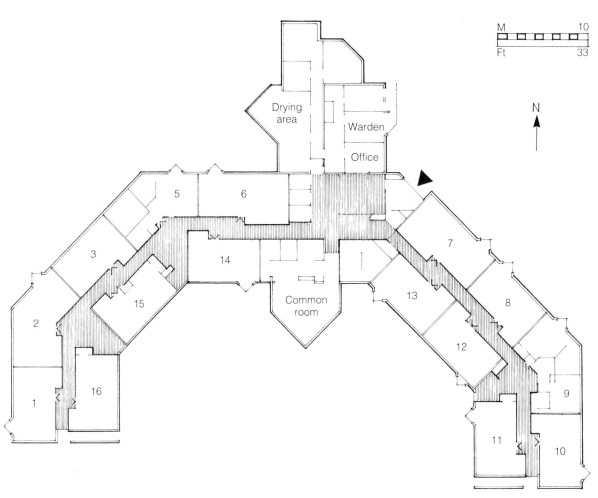

— Differentiating wall, ceiling and floors by colour and texture, and picking out features such as skirting boards and door frames will also lessen the likelihood of disorientation.

— Whilst the use of fluorescent strip lighting is accepted as the most economical form of lighting, from a maintenance point of view it can enforce an institutional atmosphere, especially when mounted centrally on corridor ceilings. Consideration should be given to other forms of low energy lighting which perhaps may be wall-mounted. The highlighting of node points such as flat entrances also helps to break down the scale of the corridor. However, the lighting design should ensure adequate illumination of all circulation areas, bearing in mind the problems that accompany the failing eyesight associated with ageing.

A common problem in the design of corridors is usually related to inadequate lighting, where lighting levels are based upon those which would be acceptable for most people. For an older person, the shock of moving from a dimly-lit corridor to a brightly lit room (or vice versa) can be discomforting and hazardous. Joe Jordan

— Wall finishes in corridors appear to vary from one scheme to another, ranging from simply painted plaster to wall coverings and fairfaced brickwork. However, rough-cast fairfaced brickwork should be avoided up to 1524mm (5 ft) from finished floor level, as it can graze people who fall or brush against its surface.

In order deliberately to vary the circulation spaces, not only vertically from floor to floor but also horizontally along the corridor, the design should perhaps utilise a whole palette of finishes, to create a varied but very much co-ordinated appearance and provide a series of visual and tactile aids to orientation.

— The carpet is the most popular form of floor finish, although the use of quarry tiles to emphasis the 'street' has been successful.

— An essential feature of the circulation routes will be a handrail fixed on both sides of the corridor at a height of 900mm (3 ft). For those residents with failing eyesight, it will be important that the handrail can easily be distinguished from the rest of the wall, and for all residents it should be easy to grasp.

Vertical circulation

The position of the stairs and lifts should be clearly marked and designed as a nodal point in the circulation area. Any scheme above one storey should have a lift within easy access of each dwelling. The lift must be considered as part

Key dimensions to main corridor elevation.

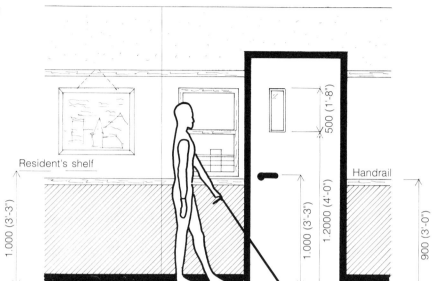
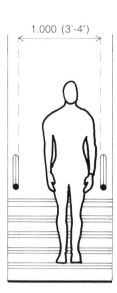

Resident's shelf

Handrail

Key dimensions to staircases. Local building codes should be checked for compliance with fire and safety regulations.

See lower illustration on p. 81 for lighting.

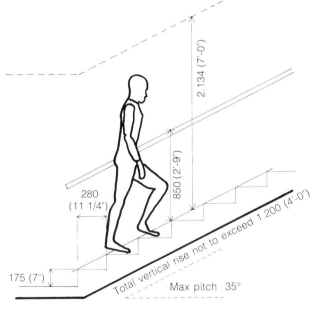

280
(11 1/4")

175 (7")

Total vertical rise not to exceed 1:200 (4'-0")

Max pitch 35°

Key dimensions at lift controls for wheelchair user.

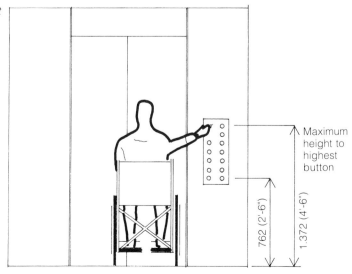

Maximum height to highest button

Key dimensions to life/elevator layout with extension facility.

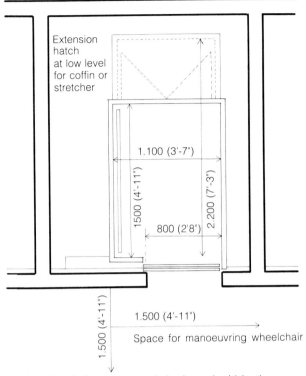

Extension hatch at low level for coffin or stretcher

1.100 (3'-7")

1.500 (4'-11")

800 (2'8")

2.200 (7'-3")

1.500 (4'-11")

1.500 (4'-11")

Space for manoeuvring wheelchair

of the circulation area and designed within the same constraints. A lift may cause anxiety to some residents not used to its operation, so it is important that it should be easy to operate, and have floor numbers clearly defined. Handrails should be provided on all sides of the lift. The lift should also be programmed to stay open long enough to allow for wheelchair users to pass in and out, to close slowly, and to be touch-sensitive, so as to reopen in the event of a person not clearing the doors in time. The position of the controls should also allow for operation by wheelchair users. In case of emergency, the lift should be included within the overall alarm system; it should also be fitted with a fold-down chair. A minimum of two lifts should be con-sidered, in case one fails. The lift should certainly be large enough to take a wheelchair user plus, of course, another person who may well be the care assister. An extension facility should also be considered, for occasional use in carrying furni-ture or a stretcher. Stairs will of course need to conform to building regulations and codes. Geof-frey Salmon recommends that:

Widths should not exceed 1m (3 ft 4 in) with con-tinuous handrail position on both sides[5].

As with the corridors, it will be an advantage to provide small seating areas at the half-landings, to allow residents to rest.
— Good shadowless light, natural, if possible, is essential for staircases, with handrails being clearly distinguishable. Nosings should also be clearly marked, and the top and bottom of each flight distinguished from the landing and the other steps. Colour differentiation between treads and risers should also be considered.

Communal and Shared Use Facilities

Perhaps the main distinguishing feature of housing designed specifically for elderly people, as opposed to general housing, is its inclusion of communal and shared use facilities. These include designated rooms or spaces within the development which residents may share or use together for a whole range of activities. Earlier projects did not always possess such facilities. However, as the process of ageing and its implications have become better understood, so communal facilities have expanded and have become an increasingly important component in housing for elderly people.

Since the first programs of research carried out in the United States some fifteen years ago, I have noted that if opportunities do not exist then the social activity of a development's population can actually decline. This results as residents begin, perhaps through their increasing disability, to

become more isolated, first from the wider community and then from other residents. We therefore need to take even twice as seriously the possibility of designing-in spaces where social contact and behaviour can develop out of natural traffic and functional use of spaces.
Dr M. Powell Lawton

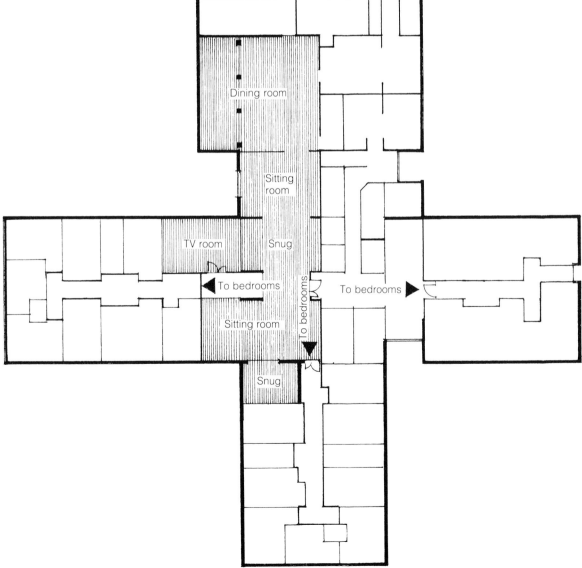

At Mount Pleasant Lane a sliding partition (which can be used by residents) allows for flexibility if more than one type of activity is anticipated (architects: Anthony Richardson and Partners).

The quiet room for reading at BUPA House.

A galleried lounge area provides for views from a smaller sitting space at first floor to the main lounge area on the ground floor at Daventry, UK (architects, and illustration: Phippen Randall Parkes).

③

Peter Phippen has also explained the importance of communal facilities in relation to the ageing process.

For the active elderly, communal facilities may not be so necessary. But with the gradual but inevitable loss of ability which accompanies ageing it will not be long before the active elderly become more frail and lose the ability to go outside to meet other people, to visit friends or to cook the necessary food to sustain a proper diet.

Even for those who may still be able to venture out and to cook their own meals, the communal facilities should provide the opportunity to socialise, but should do so in a very unobtrusive way. The variety of human behaviour transcends age. There will always, therefore, be those who prefer by choice to keep themselves to themselves. Hence it should not be assumed that as one becomes older one becomes obliged to socialise, any more or less than throughout the rest of one's life. Of course, as one grows older so one's friends, relations and spouses may pass away; but as Butler Oldman and Greve found in their studies it cannot be assumed that any sense of loneliness or isolation will be overcome merely by grouping people of the same age together[6]. At best, therefore, good design can encourage social interaction; it cannot enforce it.

Communal facilities

Communal facilities may be described under the following general headings:
Seating areas.
Dining areas.
Service facilities.

Seating areas

Activity
Unlike the other spaces in the building (the dwellings, and the circulation areas), the sitting areas will be used largely out of choice. Earlier schemes tended to provide one large room on the ground floor where residents were expected to sit and talk and to socialise. However such spaces, without adequate sub-division, can be uncomfortable to be in, especially for small groups of people or even for an individual. Also, their proportions did not reflect the more domestic image of a lounge, a far more appropriate image to project than that of a common room.

Continuing the theme of providing as rich and as varied an environment as possible, especially for those residents who may become building-bound, a variety of sitting areas in terms of size and character should therefore be considered, rather than just one large room.

You need to allow for the development of a social centre within the building, but avoiding just one large, impersonal room. The number of individual

Patio area directly off main circulation route at Manston Court (architects: Architects' Department, City of Southampton).

Secondary sitting space at Mulgrave House, accessed directly off a major circulation route. This is situated adjacent to the shared kitchen and dining facilities. The space also serves to break up the corridor and thereby become an incident in the journey through the corridor (architects: Sir Lancelot Keay and Partners).

sitting areas can be arranged in some type of cluster or distributed arrangement to provide for the different kinds of activity, some of which will be quiet and solitary (like reading) or there will be people in small groups playing cards which may be relatively quiet and involve a little conversation. Some activities, however, like television watching, will generate a higher level of noise. Therefore, the degree of sensitivity of a designer is called forth particularly in the arrangements of the social spaces. You have to get beyond the known nature of a room and get into the clear visualisation of the activities that are going to occur there. Joe Jordan

Those occasions when large gatherings may take place should also be considered. In the United States many schemes, particularly life care developments, provide separate auditoria which can accommodate all residents for concerts and large meetings. Where a separate auditorium cannot be justified, then provision for adapting either the lounge area or the dining space for occasional large gatherings should be made.

Design criteria
At least one lounge should be provided, but it should be a cluster of interrelated and definable sitting spaces and not necessarily one large room. Geoffrey Salmon recommends, especially for frail elderly, that a provision (in aggregate) for sitting areas should not fall below 3.6m² (39 sq ft) per resident[7].
— The layout of the main lounge should where possible allow for even small groups of people to gather and feel comfortable.

For the main communal area it should have lots of corners which can create places for people to colonise. We now aim to provide a fireplace as a visual centre piece to help define the space. Even in large areas the use of furniture, if properly chosen, can help to define space. Peter Phippen

The location of the sitting areas should relate to a point of demand. For example, one of the main activities would be the journey to the dining room. The assembling of people before and after their

meal provides a natural opportunity for social contact.

The lounge area should ideally be placed to act as a pre-and post-function of the activity of dining. Gilbert Rosenthal

Sitting areas that do not relate to a major circulation area are going to be ill-used. People will concentrate around the nodes of circulation, whether it be where the elevator empties out or where the front door is, or where the supervisory personnel are. Joe Jordan

— The key to providing sitting areas which will be well used is to locate them adjacent to major circulation routes, and just as importantly, to relate the space itself to some form of associated activity. This is particularly significant when considering dispersed sitting areas within the building.

Dispersed lounges not associated with functional activities tend to be under-utilized. Instead, the clustering of communal areas tends to be far more successful. Joe Jordan

— A small kitchen with facilities for preparing beverages and for serving light refreshments should be next to the main lounge.
— Toilet facilities should also be nearby, with cloakrooms for visitors' hats and coats.
— In addition to the main lounge areas, secondary sitting spaces for smaller groups varying from 4 to 10 people may also be considered. This is especially true where the accommodation consists of single bedrooms for frail elderly people, where there are secondary kitchen and dining facilities shared by groups of residents. Other activities for which secondary sitting spaces may be provided are the entertaining of friends and family who come to visit, or small card-playing groups or knitting clubs. These spaces may therefore require a higher degree of privacy, but still be very much related to the larger social setting.
— It will be important for some of the secondary sitting spaces to be clustered around the main lounge. This will allow people to sit quietly

Block planning lay-out for lounge/ sitting areas.

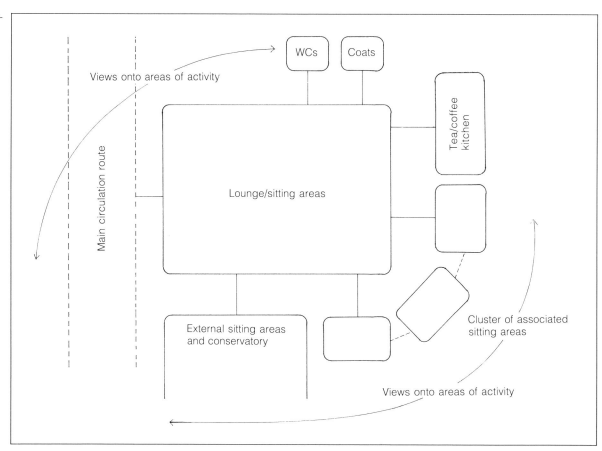

Views onto areas of activity

WCs

Coats

Tea/coffee kitchen

Main circulation route

Lounge/sitting areas

External sitting areas and conservatory

Cluster of associated sitting areas

Views onto areas of activity

At Springfield Court the sitting spaces flow from the main lounge area to the con- servatory through to an external sit- ting space. This allows for the difference types of spaces to be informally linked and not isolated from each other (architects: Milton Keynes Develop- ment Corporation).

At Waverly Heights even the nursing home wing has a shel- tered patio which can be enjoyed by those residents who may be building-bound (architects: Sulli- van Associates, photo Jim Schafer).

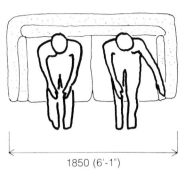

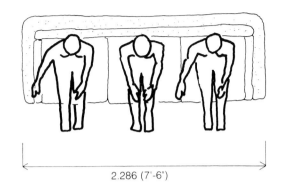

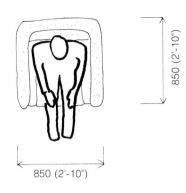

1850 (6'-1")   2.286 (7'-6")   850 (2'-10")   850 (2'-10")

Key dimensions to size of seating for communal areas. (Note: a variety of shapes and sizes is to be anticipated in residents' own rooms if they are to be allowed the opportunity of bringing their own furniture).

and observe the comings-and-goings of the main area without feeling obliged to become involved. This arrangement can even take the form of an access gallery at the first floor, which overlooks the activity of the main lounge area on the ground floor.
— When considering the smaller sitting areas, external spaces should be remembered. During fine weather a chance to sit out in a sheltered south-facing patio, perhaps off the main lounge, should be allowed for. The simple conservatory which is surprisingly little used, is a relatively cheap method of providing sheltered sitting-out spaces for those who may not wish or may not be able to venture outdoors, but nonetheless may

want to enjoy the external environment a conservatory can offer.

Dining Areas

Activity
In those schemes in which at least one hot meal is to be centrally prepared and eaten regularly by all or even a large group of residents, a separate dining area will be required. For the active elderly, facilities for preparing their own meals are an important part of their retaining their independence. However, there are important considerations to take into account which relate to possible physical or mental disabilities connected with the

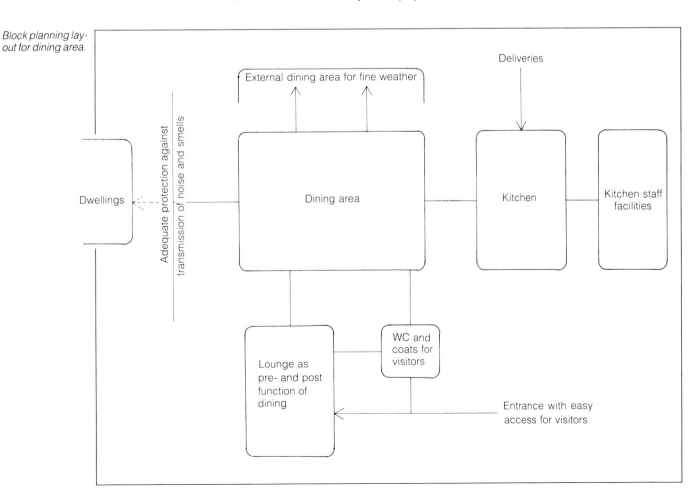

Block planning lay-out for dining area.

Key dimensions to dining room planning should include provision for wheelchair users to share table with other residents.

Dining area at Mulgrave House, East London, being used in the afternoon for a bingo session (architects: Sir Lancelot Keay and Partners).

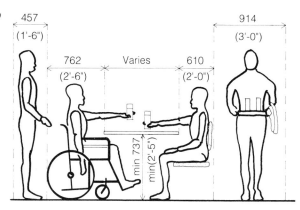

Dining rooms for elderly people do not have to have utilitarian furniture. Careful attention has been paid to the dining room at BUPA House, Milton Keynes, UK (architects: Salmon Speed). See also Waverley Heights, p. 57.

ageing process:

1 Mental frailty
As discussed in chapter 3, this can involve depression and a degree of dementia. This can lead either to the lack of willpower to prepare meals (and hence to failure to eat the correct type of food), or to the actual preparation of meals becoming in itself a hazardous task.

2 Physical frailty
This can involve the simple inability to hold appliances firmly or to move about the kitchen, and just as important, the ability to go out and shop for food. Even in those schemes where it is

At Golda Meir House, Newton, Mass., USA, residents choose to linger after their meal to have coffee or to play cards. The area is therefore well utilized throughout the day (Architects: Larkin Glassman and Prager).

Meal preparation at Help the Aged's the Mount, Woking, UK. The kitchen is equipped for preparation of diet meals, which are particularly important for residents in the nursing home section.

meal they may wish to linger, either in the dining room itself or in a nearby lounge.

The location, setting and facilities of the dining area will therefore need to be sensitive to this, to make the taking of meals as enjoyable an experience as possible.

Some schemes have also introduced luncheon clubs, in which elderly residents who live in the local area are invited to take meals with residents, thereby extending the potential for social interaction with people outside the building. Both in the United States and the United Kingdom, an increasing number of schemes are undertaking this idea and operating it on a self-financing basis. One particularly successful scheme is the Lord Gage Centre, East London, operated by the Guinness Trust.

We provide up to 70 lunches a day, 5 days a week, for elderly people in the local borough. People come not only for the meal but for the company and friendship it brings. Christine Hunt, Special Projects Officer, the Guiness Trust

The inviting of elderly non-residents applies equally to all ranges of the market. In the United States many life care communities open their restaurants to non-residents, to allow for a greater social interaction with a wider community and to extend the opportunity for potential residents to experience at first hand the benefits and facilities of moving to that development.

assumed that residents can cook for themselves, this capacity will inevitably deteriorate over time. Meals can of course be centrally prepared, on or off site, and delivered to individual dwellings.

However, because of the importance of the need to shape the day, as Dr Anne Roberts explained in chapter 3, lunch and dinner can become important parts of that day.

Dining, therefore, is not just the activity of eating a meal. It is instead a setting for social interaction which can become the main focal point to a resident's day. Residents will tend to congregate around the dining area up to one or even two hours before meals are served. This will be to meet friends and converse. Even after the

Suggested layout for the kitchen and stores for 20–25 residents by Geoffrey Salmon from the Abbeyfield Extra Care Manual *1982, the Abbeyfield Society, St Albans, Herts.*[4]

1 Hot cupboard
2 Open shelf unit
3 Water boiler
4 Stainless steel table
5 Dishwasher
6 Double bowl sink unit
7 Potato peeler
8 Cupboard (stainless steel top)
9 Mixer
10 Stainless steel handbasin
11 Refrigerator
12 Freezer
13 Gas oven and grill
14 Double fryer
15 Steamer
16 Cooker hood
17 Heated trolleys

18 Racking
19 Vegetable rack
20 Three-tier trolley
21 Chest freezer
22 Refuse sack holder

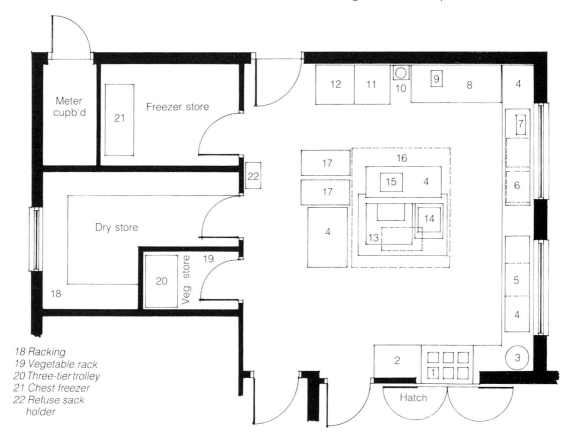

Design criteria
— Space allowances will need to take account of residents having to negotiate their way past the tables and chairs in wheelchairs or walking aids. Geoffrey Salmon recommends a minimum of 2.6 sq m (28 sq ft) per resident[9]. This would need to be increased should the anticipated operational policy be to serve non-residents.
— The kitchen should be designed to allow for preparation of special diet meals. The policy of meal preparation (i.e. the need for a hot cupboard or freezer if pre-cooked or frozen meals are to be used) should be determined during the design stage of the kitchen, as this will determine its size. Specialist advice, ideally from the user group, should also be sought on the exact layout of the kitchen.
— The dining area should enjoy direct access from the kitchen and, like the common room, should be adjacent to WCs and cloakrooms.
— Consideration should be given to the dining room also being used for large gatherings of residents, as for parties, bingo sessions or large meetings.
— The noise, and sometimes the smells, of a busy kitchen imply that it should be sited away from the residents' dwellings to avoid the possible nuisance. Separate facilities for staff using the kitchen must also be provided. Local hygiene regulations and codes will also need to be considered at the design stage.
— The kitchen area will also need its own service entrance for daily deliveries.

Service facilities

The post room

Activity
As the ability to visit friends and family may diminish, or as those friends and family themselves age, the personal letter assumes a greater significance as a means of communicating with those outside the building. The telephone is of course a vital link, but with time to spare, letters can become treasured items. In many American schemes this has been interpreted into making the delivery of the post a communal activity. Once or twice a day residents will gather around the mail boxes waiting for the post to arrive. Then they will sit and read their letters and tell each other about their family's news, or proudly display photographs. As well as being of benefit in receiving good news, the opportunity of companionship can also comfort when letters bring problems or anxieties, such as claim benefit forms and so on.

The common post facility serves as a functionally related opportunity for residents to congregate at regular times to collect their mail. It is also a purposeful socialising function to come to a central facility to witness the bulletin board. It would be comparatively easy to deliver mail to the housing units, but we chose not to do that and instead provided the opportunity for social contact. Andrew Sullivan.

Block planning layout for post room.

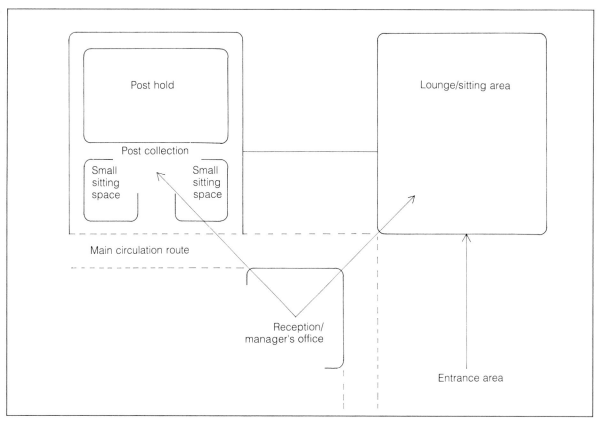

Post room at Golda Meir House, Newton, Mass., USA (architects: Larkin Glassman and Prager). The communal post facility serves as a functionally related opportunity for residents to congregate at regular times to collect their mail.

It has been noted that in cases where residents may be unable to leave their own room, care assistants or fellow residents will collect mail on a resident's behalf and bring it to their room. Assistance is also offered in a similar way in reading out and explaining the contents of a letter to those unable to read because of failing eyesight.

Design criteria
— The post room should be on the ground floor, convenient to the main entrance point, to allow residents to check mail before leaving the building, and should be immediately adjacent to the main circulation route.
— The area should allow some visual supervision from the warden/manager's office or reception desk.
— The type of mail boxes will depend upon management policy. Individual locked boxes offer security, but they would need to be easy to operate.
— The mail boxes should be so arranged that they can be reached easily by the residents. Each box should clearly show the resident's name or flat number.
— To allow an opportunity for social contact, seats should be arranged near the boxes, so that residents may wait for their post and remain in the room to read any letters.
— The seating zone could be combined with one of the lounge areas near the central entrance. If separate facilities are planned, approximately one seat per every 8 residents should be allowed for.

— This area could also serve as a suitable place for displays on the notice board and for central information.

Laundry

Activity
The activity of residents washing their clothes can be an important part of the weekly routine. The first generation of housing for elderly in the United Kingdom provided only drying areas, on the assumption that residents would hand wash their laundry or simply use the local launderette. Later schemes included a communal laundry for use by residents.

Central laundry room operated by staff at the Leonard Pulham House, Halton, Bucks., UK (architects: Salmon Speed).

Beauty parlour at Golda Meir House, Mass., USA (architects: Larkin Glassman and Prager).

The use of public laundries seems to be declining among younger generations, as the use of domestic washing machines increases. It cannot therefore be assumed that the provision of a communal laundry in a scheme will always satisfy the expectations of future users, even though existing residents may find such facilities an improvement on their previous clothes-washing arrangements. Many residents now moving to developments, especially in the private sector, may therefore have been accustomed to having their own washing machine and tumble dryer in their kitchen. They will therefore no doubt expect to see a similar facility in their new dwelling.

For the frail elderly it will be their own physical disability rather than the advent of new technology that will render the communal laundry obsolete. It cannot be assumed that even active elderly will always be able to walk to the communal laundry, or carry their washing.

Schemes designed specifically for older elderly therefore tend not to include a communal laundry, and instead laundry is either dealt with by staff on site or handled by a commercial laundry service off site.

Design criteria
— The alternatives to be considered in providing laundry facilities will therefore be:
1 To allow additional space in the resident's kitchen for a plumbed-in washing machine/ tumble dryer.
2 To provide for residents who may wish to use shared laundry facilities.
3 To provide for all laundry to be processed on site by a central laundry service operated by staff.
4 To provide for a part of that laundry (such as bed linen) to be processed off site by a commercial service.
— If shared facilities are provided they should include sinks, washing machines and tumble dryers. These should be domestic models and hence easy to operate. A worktop for ironing and folding should also be provided. To deal with flooding, there should be adequate drainage, ideally with a floor drain. Machines should stand on a plinth 250mm (10″) high to save users bending down to load them.
— In any shared use facility, sizing and siting are critical. If a shared laundry room is too distant for residents, this will at best lead to frustration, and at worst deter residents from using the facility at all. The number of machines will depend upon whether management policy is able to stagger their use. However, a minimum of two 3.5kg (8 lb) washing machines and two 4.5kg (9 lb) tumble dryers per 30 dwellings should be allowed.
— For on-site central laundry facilities the capacity will depend upon the type of machines for use. Specialist advice is therefore required in the specification and layout of this facility.

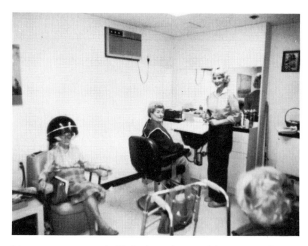

However, as an initial planning guide approximately 0.8m^2 (8 sq ft) per dwelling should be allowed for. This will include space for linen and storage.
— For both shared and staff laundry facilities the services should be washable, with a non-slip floor and adequate ventilation.
— The laundry should be conveniently sited for deliveries and pickups by the commercial laundry service, and have easy access to an outside drying area. A small sitting space adjacent to the shared facilities should be considered, as people may not wish to remain in the laundry area for the duration of the wash. Laundries produce noise and smells. They should therefore be planned so as not to cause a nuisance to residents' dwellings.

Hairdressing/beauty parlour

Activity
Many developments have included a room in which residents may have their hair washed and cut. A common error is also to allocate this space as a hobbies room when it is not in use for hairdressing. This can in practice lead to the room's being under-utilized, as it is unable successfully to fulfill both functions.

Instead, the hairdressing facility should not necessarily be viewed as a room but more as a shop. This then takes on the familiar and established image of the beauty parlour. As such, its location should not be as in some earlier schemes at the end of a corridor or on an upper floor but instead on the ground floor directly off the main circulation route. As a walk-in shop the facility can also bring with it the opportunity for social contact, like that in its High Street counterpart. The shop can then alternate from gents' to ladies' hairdressing on a day-to-day or week-to-week basis.

Design criteria
Provision should be made for a room of approximately 14m^2 (150 sq ft) on the ground floor, directly off a major circulation route and, ideally,

Mulgrave House, East London, managed by the Guinness Trust. The sitting room with its balcony is where neighbours at Mulgrave House can meet and is used in addition to the main lounge area on the ground floor.

adjoining other communal facilities.

— The more the room resembles and can function as a small hairdressing shop (i.e. with waiting chairs and back-washing facilities) the more it will be used by residents.

For example, at Golda Meir House, Newton, Massachusetts, a professional hairdresser uses the facility on a contract basis and charges her clients. This beauty parlour is well liked and well used by residents, many of whom call in just to chat. The room also doubles as a barber shop on other occasions, when the men will call or congregate to discuss sport and exchange their own news. This shop thus forms an important component of social life of the scheme.

Bedrooms	Dining — Kitchen	Bedrooms
	Circulation route	
Bedrooms	Lounge/sitting area	Bedrooms

Block planning layout for secondary dining/kitchen/ sitting areas arranged in 'family groups'.

The small dining area becomes an informal space for social interaction during morning coffee or afternoon tea.

The kitchen is used either by residents or care assistants who prepare light meals or beverages.

Secondary kitchen and dining facilities

Activity

As discussed in chapter 3, the mental and physical frailty or even temporary disability resulting from a fall can mean a person requires assistance with the preparation of meals and eating. There are schemes such as Mulgrave House, East London, where, rather than allow frail elderly residents to become totally dependent upon outside help, secondary kitchen and dining facilities allow them to support each other, with staff assisting as necessary. Residents may prepare their own breakfasts, light meals and beverages as they please and therefore still maintain that essential degree of control. Mulgrave House, part of the Lord Gage Centre, is run by the Guiness Trust and provides a total of 30 single rooms which are grouped at 10 per floor, over three floors. Each family group, as it is called, has its own lounge, dining room, kitchen and assisted bathroom. The arrangement and policy of the building is to allow each resident to maintain as independent a way of life as possible.

The appeal of the family group concept is that it allows the scale of development to be broken down and smaller neighbourhoods to be identified.

Design criteria

— Shared facilities should be identified with a defined number of dwellings, to promote the sense that each set belongs to its group of users. Anonymous facilities off a corridor which appear to belong to no-one should be avoided.

— The kitchen should also be designed to allow residents to prepare their own beverages and light snacks; the travel distance between it and their dwelling should therefore be kept to a minimum. A kitchen size of approximately 10m^2 (107 sq ft) should be sufficient to serve a family group of 10 bed sitting rooms.

— The secondary dining and sitting areas should be clustered round the secondary kitchen area and reached off the main circulation route to the adjoining dwellings. Their sizing will relate to the number in the family group, but with an additional allowance for visitors, who may include other residents in the scheme.

Shared use facilities

Shared use facilities also include those areas which may be used individually (that is, not communally) by any resident or authorised visitor to the building.

Assisted personal washing spaces

Activity

Physical or mental frailty, or even a temporary disability, can also cause a person to require assistance with washing and toilet functions. Because of the importance of being able to maintain and support an individual's dignity and privacy, even assisted washing should ideally be undertaken inside their dwelling. However, if they are unable to get in or out of a bath, this will necessitate a degree of mechanical assistance to ensure this can be done safely and without undue stress on both bather and helper. The expense and the space needed for such specialist mechanical equipment will dictate that the facilities have to be shared. This will entail the resident's having to leave their dwelling to be bathed. Many residents may, of course, require assistance in using the toilet. In the United States, opinion

Plan of Mulgrave House showing the family group layout, with shared facilities clustered round the resident's dwellings (architects: Sir Lancelot Keay and Partners).

Layout of assisted bathroom based on the recommendations of the Scottish Housing Handbook, Housing for the Elderly[6]. reproduced with the permission of the Controller of HMSO.

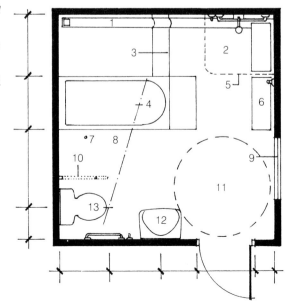

1 Drainage channel
2 Possible position of shower
3 Possible steps to sunken area for assistant to stand
4 Line of hoist
5 Curtain
6 Folding seat
7 Pole
8 Slot under for feet of hoist
9 Window located for ease of access
10 Hinged grabrail
11 Wheelchair turning space
12 Basin suitable for washing hair
13 WC

Different types of assisted bath and shower arrangements.

—

Medic Bath functions as a walk-in bath where the bather sits in first and the bath then fills. Manufactured by Medic-Bath Ltd.

Hi-Lo assisted bath can be raised to a comfortable working height for a nurse or attendant. Manufactured by Mecanaids Ltd.

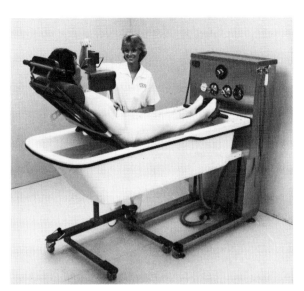

Assisted bath assembly with hoist for lifting bathers in and out of a bath. Manufactured by Caradon Twyfords Ltd.

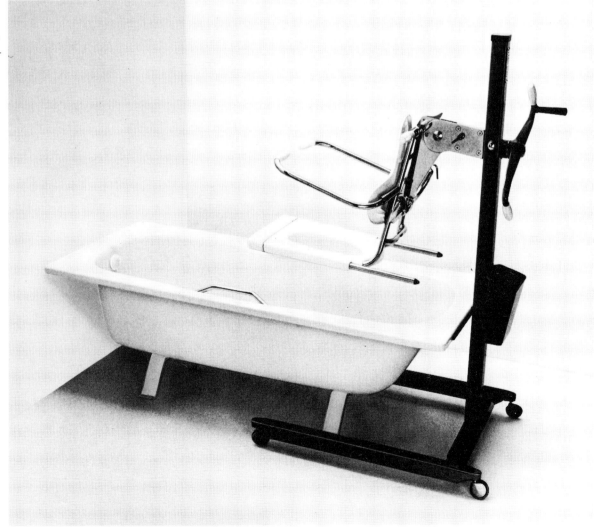

Shower cubicle with fold-down seat. The need to provide barrier free access to the shower tray is sometimes incompatible with the technical requirement to provide adequate drainage and gulley access. This is one solution which incorporates a slightly raised but ramped access to the shower tray without the need to unnecessarily complicate drainage/access. Manufactured by J.W. Swain Plastics Ltd.

amongst gerontologists, behavioural scientists and private developers is firmly in favour of retaining a toilet facility within a resident's dwelling (see pp. 102, 104).

The number of people, despite their state of health, who would thrive on having to share a toilet who could afford or choose something else, would be very small. Dr M. Powell Lawton

Design criteria

— Assuming each dwelling as a minimum have its own WC and shower, a ratio of one assisted bath per 25 residents, or ideally one on each floor should be considered.

— It should be noted that even in those schemes designed specifically for the younger active elderly, the inevitability of ageing will mean that some residents will require assistance in bathing. Though personal care services can be brought into the building, their effectiveness will invariably depend upon the facilities available. As the private market develops and user expectations become more sophisticated, the attractiveness of the scheme may be compromised if it lacks the basic facility for assisted bathing when required.

— The bathroom should be designed to accommodate a free-standing bath to allow assistance on both sides[10]

— The bath should be to a specialist design, allowing a person to be transferred to the bath without having to be lifted by the helper. There is a growing range of such baths and medical/

nurse/client representatives should be consulted as to the most appropriate choice[11].

— The assisted bathroom should also include a WC and walk-in shower. There appears to be mixed opinion as to a shower's popularity, particularly in the United Kingdom. Whilst showers do avoid the effort of having to negotiate a person into a bath, they are less convenient for assisted washing. As the use of showers becomes more established in the United Kingdom amongst younger generations, no doubt showers will become more popular amongst future generations of elderly people.

— Floor finishes should of course be non-slip and washable. However, despite the utilitarian function of the assisted bath and WC, this area will still represent part of the resident's home. The decoration of these rooms should therefore be sensitive to this.

— As with all bathroom design it will be important to avoid the problems caused by excessive condensation.

— WCs should also be planned by the entrance area, the common lounge and the dining room. Again, the need to provide for wheelchair access will be important.

Medicloo acts as a washer/dryer bidet facility and can be adapted to most existing or new standard WC suites. It allows for greater independence and privacy in personal hygiene when required. Manufactured by Medic-Bath Ltd.

The Parker bath, another option for walk-in baths. Manufactured by Parker Bath Developments Ltd.

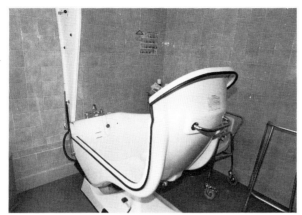

Short-stay accommodation

Activity
In developments which consist mainly of single bedroom or bed-sit dwellings there will be a need to provide additional short-stay accommodation for use by the following:
—   Prospective residents who may wish to assess the development and its facilities before moving in.
—   Temporary residents who may stay in the development while their own family takes a holiday.
—   Temporary residents who may stay during a short period of convalescence.
—   Guests who may be visiting relatives and require overnight accommodation.
—   Residents whose flat may be temporarily out of service, e.g. while it is being decorated or repaired.

Design criteria
A minimum of one room which can hold twin beds and a washhand basin (approximately 12m^2 (40 sq ft) area) should be provided per 30 residents.
—   Each overnight room should be next to a WC and bath, which need not exclusive to that room or rooms.

Dwelling Units: the Private Living Spaces

One of the key distinguishing features which differentiates a person's home from an institution is the sense that one has control over what one does within it. It can be a place of refuge from the worries and uncertainties of the outside world. Above all, it is the one place where a person can entirely and exclusively be himself or herself. The ageing process may well infringe upon the sacred boundaries of privacy and dignity; in designing the private living spaces, therefore, the designer should try to prevent this last refuge of independence from being invaded prematurely.

Since where a person lives will probably be where he or she will spend the most time, the precise layout of the living unit will be critical in maintaining the well-being of a scheme's residents.

The intimate environment of late life can have a profound effect on health and morale[12]. *Sandra Howell.*

To be sensitive to the activity patterns of how elderly people would expect to use their living spaces, their own environment history should be considered.

Most new residents will be moving into smaller accommodation than they have been used to. This applies even to the lower income groups. Howell estimates that in the United States the area of the average prior residence was 140m^2 (1500 sq ft), whereas the average one-bedroom unit for elderly people is 51m^2 (550 sq ft)[13]. There therefore appears, as Howell explains, to be a conflict between the planned dwelling unit for elderly people and the residents' need for an environment which will be as much of a home as possible, and in which a previously established lifestyle is supported and continued.

Two points about what happens in the living environment are also important:
— Older people (as discussed in chapter 3) will vary considerably in their lifestyles and needs, both emotionally, physically and environmentally.
— Because they may have to spend an increasing amount of time within the home, there will be a need to provide variety within the living area, as a stimulus.

Despite the provision of communal spaces, it cannot be assumed that they can necessarily compensate at all for the confinement of the dwelling unit.

Depending upon the level of care and support appropriate for the type of elderly people to be accommodated, the size and types of dwellings will tend to vary. There appear to be three generic types of dwelling units found in housing for elderly people:
Single bed unit
Bed-sit or efficiency unit
Apartments with separate bedrooms

Single-bed unit

This is usually a room of approximately 14m^2 (150 sq ft) area. This type of accommodation is usually provided specifically for single, frail elderly people who require a high level of nursing or care assistance (see chapter 1 for a definition of nursing care and residential care). If it is for nursing care accommodation this type of accom-

At BUPA House, Milton Keynes, England, residents in single bed units may bring their own furniture, to provide an essential link with their past (architects: Salmon Speed).

Key dimensions to access around beds.

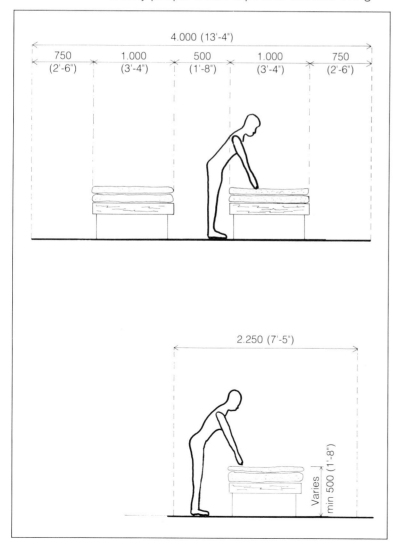

The self-contained residential care unit with basic kitchen equipment. Many gerontologists, in both the United States and United Kingdom, would prefer such an arrangement even in the extra care facilities, rather than the singe bed unit in which a kitchen or WC has to be shared. Layout based upon studio flats at the Mount (architects: Hutchinson Lock and Monk).

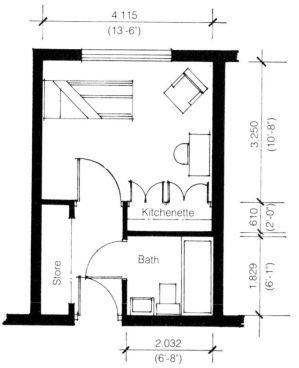

modation may not include any cooking facilities, but it should still have its own WC and shower. Within certain life care projects the single bed unit may be used on a short-term basis, when a resident may warrant additional nursing super vision, but could later move back to their own apartment within the life care community, or outside the facility, when sufficiently recovered.

Activity
Residents of single-bed units may, by definition, not be capable of preparing their own food, may well need assistance to walk to the WC and may not be able to use it without help. In short, they would require assistance with all the activities of daily living. The serving of main meals in a central dining area will provide an important incentive for a journey to the dining room, for those able to manage it. The majority of a resident's time might, however, be spent in their own room: either in a chair or in bed watching television or listening to the radio, reading, or just sitting.

Design criteria
— The importance of making it possible for

Single-bed accommodation should also provide for 'linking' rooms to provide two-bed units for those residents who choose to share accommodation, within a nursing or residential care setting. The curtain track is used to maintain privacy during attendance by staff.

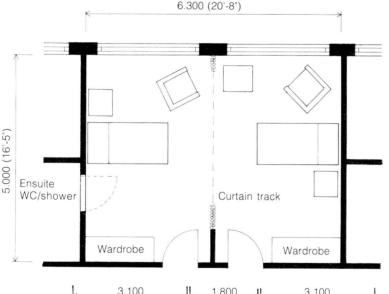

Single-bed nursing unit with ensuite WC planned to allow double-banking of service outlets.

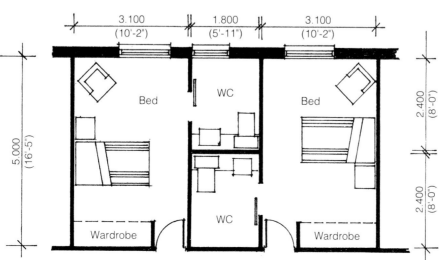

At Leonard Pulham House the low window sill allows residents to enjoy the view out, from either a chair or the bed (Architects: Salmon Speed).

secure in their own private space.

— Because residents in single bed units may have to spend large parts of the day in bed, it will be important to allow the view out from the window to be visible from a lying position.

— Common to all private living spaces will be the need to allow residents to bring with them their own items of furniture from their previous home. This is a great source of comfort and helps with the identification of a resident's immediate environment (see chapter 3).

There can of course be a conflict here, in that while the resident of a single-bed unit may benefit greatly by being able to retain personal items of furniture linking their new home with their past, the space available for this may clearly be limited, and nursing licensing standards may well militate against the potential cluttering of a room with too much of resident's furniture.

— This conflict may be reduced where units are used on a short-term basis, for example by allowing residents to bring their own photographs or paintings to their room to implant a limited sense of personal identity.

— Whilst it is accepted that most frail residents of single-bed units will always require assistance with washing and using the toilet, opinion, particularly in the United States, is very much in favour of each resident still possessing their own WC. After her extensive research in the field, Sandra Howell questions the long-term suitability of single-bed units without an en-suite toilet facility.

residents to see out from their room onto a varied and active view therefore assumes a greater importance, since the single bed unit cannot in itself provide such variety. The view out can of course be onto the outside world, as well as onto the comings-and-goings of the corridor. The high level of staff activity for frail elderly can in itself provide something interesting to watch. It should be noted that the door recess in the corridors discussed on pp. 78–80 make room for people to sit just outside their room without disturbing or obstructing the duties of the staff.

— In many single-bed schemes, residents tend to leave their door open to achieve this important sense of contact with the rest of the building, whilst at the same time remaining

It will be important to maintain the ability to see out from the window from all standing, sitting or lying positions, while at the same time ensuring a resident's privacy and security by not over-sizing the windows.

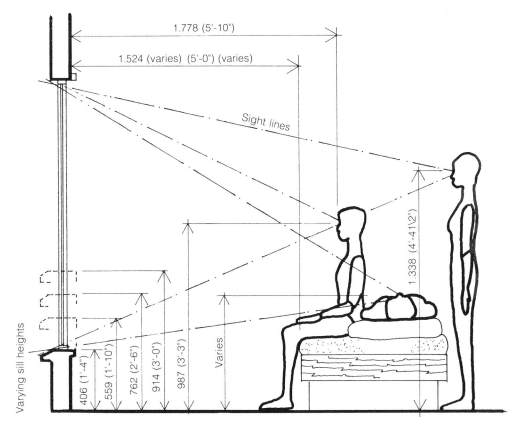

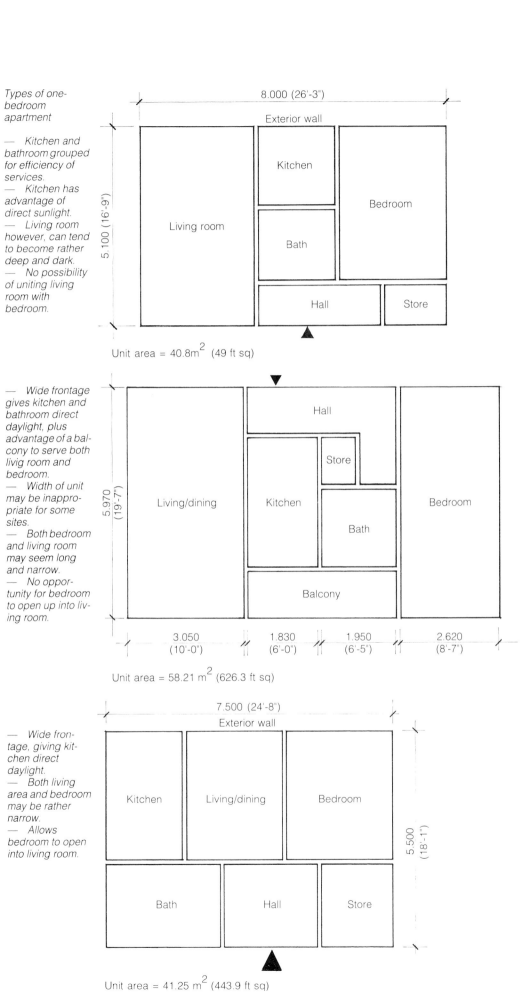

Types of one-bedroom apartment

— Kitchen and bathroom grouped for efficiency of services.
— Kitchen has advantage of direct sunlight.
— Living room however, can tend to become rather deep and dark.
— No possibility of uniting living room with bedroom.

8.000 (26'-3")
Exterior wall
Living room
Kitchen
Bath
Bedroom
Hall
Store
5.100 (16'-9")

Unit area = 40.8m^2 (49 ft sq)

— Wide frontage gives kitchen and bathroom direct daylight, plus advantage of a balcony to serve both livig room and bedroom.
— Width of unit may be inappropriate for some sites.
— Both bedroom and living room may seem long and narrow.
— No opportunity for bedroom to open up into living room.

Hall
Store
Living/dining
Kitchen
Bath
Bedroom
Balcony
5.970 (19'-7")

3.050 (10'-0")   1.830 (6'-0")   1.950 (6'-5")   2.620 (8'-7")

Unit area = 58.21 m^2 (626.3 ft sq)

— Wide frontage, giving kitchen direct daylight.
— Both living area and bedroom may be rather narrow.
— Allows bedroom to open into living room.

7.500 (24'-8")
Exterior wall
Kitchen
Living/dining
Bedroom
Bath
Hall
Store
5.500 (18'-1")

Unit area = 41.25 m^2 (443.9 ft sq)

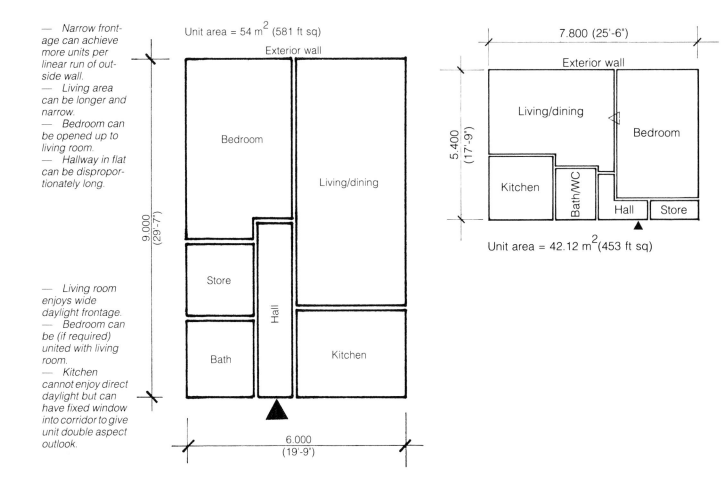

— Narrow front-
age can achieve
more units per
linear run of out-
side wall.
— Living area
can be longer and
narrow.
— Bedroom can
be opened up to
living room.
— Hallway in flat
can be dispropor-
tionately long.

— Living room
enjoys wide
daylight frontage.
— Bedroom can
be (if required)
united with living
room.
— Kitchen
cannot enjoy direct
daylight but can
have fixed window
into corridor to give
unit double aspect
outlook.

Unit area = 54 m^2 (581 ft sq)
Exterior wall
Bedroom
Living/dining
Store
Hall
Bath
Kitchen
9.000 (29'-7")
6.000 (19'-9")

7.800 (25'-6")
Exterior wall
Living/dining
Bedroom
Kitchen
Bath/WC
Hall
Store
5.400 (17'-9")
Unit area = 42.12 m^2 (453 ft sq)

*There are probably populations of older and
frailer elderly for whom the unit without its own
WC is a suitable solution. I think in many cases
the absence of a toilet in your own unit, particularly for the frailer elderly, is not a good idea. A
toilet facility is more than just a psychological
issue. As people get older and frailer, their ability
to control their bowel and bladder functions
decreases. There is therefore an increased need
to take care of their body functions both day and
night. The issue of sharing a WC is therefore not
conducive to respecting a resident's privacy and
dignity, both physiologically and psychologically.
Sandra Howell.*

The need for individual toilets and cooking facilities, even in extra care developments, was also
recommended by the working party of Age Concern which reported in 1984[14].

Dr M. Powell Lawton has also commented on
this issue:

*An aspect of learning from the environment is
controlling the environment. This is very closely
related to preserving a person's dignity and
psychological indepence and well-being. To be
able to retain a basic kitchen facility and*
*bathroom, even if their use becomes difficult or
impossible without assistance, is psychologically
important. It is a familiar ingredient to one's
domestic environment.
The absence of even a small cooking facility for
residential as opposed to nursing care units,
even just to heat water for tea or soup, is a constraint on the freedom of the elderly resident.*

*The main questions must be whether, without
these basic amenities, the living unit is really
supportive to independence and autonomy, and
whether coming generations of elderly will accept
that kind of constraint? I suspect this is not the
direction in which people are going. Instead, we
are moving towards a smaller version of what they
have lived in most of their lives, and this includes
the older and frailer elderly. Sandra Howell.*

— Because of the legal requirement in both the
USA and the UK to register both residential and
nursing accommodation with the local health or
housing authorities, early consultation should be
sought with the licensing representatives, to
ensure that the facilities planned comply with
local codes and standards.

Bed-sit or efficiency unit

This would normally be a self-contained combined living/eating/sleeping arrangement, with an approximate minimum gross floor area of 32m² (350 sq ft). The unit would be self-contained with its own kitchen area and bath/WC and would be mostly for single people.

Dr Anne Roberts believes that this type of accommodation is particularly suitable when considering extra care facilities.

With the increase in the proportion of frail elderly people, then the idea of providing only self-contained flats will become less appropriate. The demand for these elderly will be towards the bed-sitting type of dwelling, with minimal cooking facilities but grouped around shared kitchens which may be used independently or assisted, as appropriate. Dr Anne Roberts (see also page 95).

Activity
The activities of the residents of efficiency apartments will be similar to those in the single-bed units, but the more active elderly would be able to manage a more independent lifestyle.

Accepting the fact that the single-bed unit will be designed as an aid to maintaining a degree of independence for the frail elderly, the bed-sit or efficiency has the advantage of being adaptable to frail single elderly, but can have the disadvantage of not representing a conventional living pattern for the active elderly. This is particularly seen in the use of the same space for living and sleeping.

Sleeping necessitates a high degree of privacy and security. It takes place in a personal space where a person's most treasured or personal belongings may be kept, as well as their clothing or bedside medicine. Open views of the bed by a visitor, especially a stranger, can occur in a badly planned unit, and may well be considered taboo. They cause embarrassment and anxiety to residents.

To understand the user activities, a day in the life of one resident may be examined, more to give an indication rather than define a hard-and-fast pattern of use, since individual lifestyles can be so varied (for a more detailed analysis of user activity patterns see *Designing for Aging: Patterns of Use*)[15] (see pp.106–7)

Design criteria

Entrance area

This area is at the threshold of a resident's private territory; it is a transition zone in which the resident will greet friends and check out visitors before allowing them in. It should therefore be adequately defined, and sufficiently separated from the more private living spaces, so that visual contact with them is minimised and privacy guarded.

— Some special design attention, such as the provision of a recessed doorway or ample corridor space to hold plants, *bric-à-brac* or other ornaments, should be exercised, to express individual identity and socially attribute the front porch.

A window by the doorway or somewhere a resident may mark their porch allows for personal identification as well as giving some definition to the corridor spaces. Gilbert Rosenthal.

— A shelf by the front door serves as a place to personalise and as a useful position to leave postal or food deliveries, to save the resident from bending down to retrieve them from the floor. The shelf can also act as a support for a bag while the keys to the apartment are got out. The optimum height of the shelf would be 1000mm (3 ft 3 in).

— Inside the entrance the area should have storage, such as a closet, as well as some furnishability: a place for a small table, for packages, or for a chair to sit on while putting on boots.

Internal doors

— Clear opening widths of internal doors within the private living spaces are sometimes better reduced to a minimum of 775mm (2 ft 6½ in), as larger widths can sterilise too much floor space, especially in restricted areas.

Kitchen areas

— Research has shown that elderly persons prefer to have an area, even if minimal, for preparing and eating food in the privacy of their own dwellings. This suggests that although kitchen spaces may be planned for shared use, some provision should be made to allow minimal cooking within the dwelling for as long as a resident is capable: the design of the kitchen is discussed in more detail later in this section.

Dining

— Even within a bed-sitter there should be spaces allocated for dining. If the unit is larger, both an informal place in or close to the kitchen, and a more formal dining space are desirable.

Looking out

— As with the single-bed units, openable windows, especially in the sleeping areas, are highly desired by older people who may spend days in bed with a disability. Consideration should be given to the view from a lying position and the ease of drawing of curtains, and windows be

Cont on p. 108

Although residents may at times be unable to leave their room, there should be sufficient space to allow for other residents, staff or family and friends to visit (Courtesy Methodist Homes for the Aged).

A day in the life

Mrs Sarah Cohen is 90 years old. She originally lived in a three-bedroomed house with her husband and two children in North London, England. Her husband passed away in 1960. In 1968 she moved to her daughter's home, which was in another part of London, as she could no longer cope with maintaining her own house. Because of the difficulties of negotiating stairs in her daughter's house and the problems of overcrowding, she moved again, to a bed-sitting apartment closer to her original family home. A typical day in the life would be as follows:

Time:	Activity:
6.00am	Wakes up: time varies and can be very early if there is trouble in sleeping. Usually the first thing is to make a cup of tea and take it back to bed, or to sit in the armchair and maybe listen to the radio for an hour or two. May even go back to sleep.
8.00am	Goes to the bathroom and washes and dresses. Prepares and eats breakfast.
9.00am	House manager calls in for a chat or may call by telephone.
9.30am	Twice a week a home help will call; she will help clean the flat and bring in some shopping. She usually stays until 11.30am. Although communal dining facilities are available, Mrs Cohen prefers to cook her own lunch, which will usually consist of some soup, or meat and potatoes. She generally tends to eat her lunch alone, although her neighbours sometimes call in; or she will visit them to share lunch.
2.00pm– 5.00pm	The afternoons will generally be spent alone in the flat, either watching TV or just sitting by the window, or sometimes simply snoozing. During fine weather she will go out and do her own shopping. A favourite pastime is baking, either apple pie or biscuits.
6.30pm	House manager will call again.
7.30pm– 11.30pm	By the evening she may prepare an evening meal, but she is not always hungry enough to eat a full meal. Through the evening neighbours or visiting relatives will come by, or she will watch TV, perhaps with a neighbour.
12.00 midnight	Last thing at night Mrs Cohen enjoys a cup of hot milk and then goes to sleep.

Layout of Mrs Cohen's flat.

View of flat (note bed against the wall).

The early morning routine begins with making tea.

By midday Mrs Cohen prepares her lunch.

The afternoons may be spent watching TV or simply sitting by the window.

Her most valued possessions are her collections of family photographs spanning some four generations.

Layout of bed-sitter or efficiency unit at Claverton Court, Chester, UK, for the Architects' Benevolent Society. Note how the sleeping area may be screened off from the living area by the simple use of a curtain track. The design is also sensitive in ensuring views out from both living and sleeping areas, and even from kitchen and corridor (architects: Brock Carmichael Associates).

designed to enable a comfortable view out from a seated position as well as from the bed.

— However, there is still a need to maintain a balance between the ability to see out and the sense of security and privacy, so that a resident will not feel overlooked or exposed.

Sleeping area

— The sleeping area, as previously explained, is a personal space, and allowance should be made for residents to retain their most private memorabilia. Residents frequently wish to retain past furnishings. Space calculations should therefore allow for this, and for dressing and bed-making.

— It is therefore important to try as far as possible to visually define the sleeping area as being private territory within the bed-sit/efficiency layout. This may be achieved by various subtle devices which will not affect the barrier-free

The sleeping area can be successfully defined without compromising the advantages of the barrier-free single room layout.

advantages of a single room layout, especially for the frail resident. Examples will include:
Lowering of the ceiling above the sleeping area
Use of furniture to define the space
Changing the floor or wall finish
False ceiling beam to define and space
The ability to draw a curtain across when a visitor is present, or when a resident may need to undress, as during a doctor's visit.

Most important of all is for the sleeping area not to be seen by someone entering the flat.

Bathing facilities

— Depending upon the health of the intended resident, bathing facilities allocated may be individual or modestly congregate. In the United States, shares toilet rooms are not acceptable in a residential setting, even in extra care facilities[16].

Entertaining

— Although people may live on their own, the environment of group dwellings does mean that residents can visit each other or be visited by the warden or staff during the day. Sufficient space should therefore be provided for visitors to sit and chat, perhaps over a cup of tea or coffee. This will be particularly important during periods of illness for those residents who may become too frail to leave their own dwelling unassisted.

— As for single bed units, allowing residents an opportunity to retain some of their existing furniture will be of great benefit to them, and the layout should therefore permit a variety of furniture arrangements.

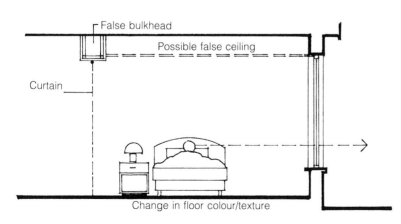

Apartments with separate bedrooms

Most sheltered and congregate housing for elderly people has been based upon one-bedroom apartments. As well as the move towards more manageable barrier-free units, particularly for frail elderly, there appears to be a rising demand for two or even three-bedroom apartments, particularly in the private sector.

Acitivity
The same basic patterns of activity would apply as for the bed-sitting units, except that the sleeping area is now in a separate room (or rooms). It is therefore closer to conventional living patterns and also allows for two persons to be accommodated.

While the one-bedroom flat can hold two persons, this is based upon the assumption that both will be able (or want) to sleep in the same room. It is here that the two bedroom layout may offer the greatest flexibility for its users. Even in the case of a married couple in which one partner is ill or suffers disturbed nights, there could be a benefit from one partner being able to sleep at least temporarily in the second bedroom. More importantly, where friends, brothers or sisters choose to live together, perhaps where their spouses have passed away, a two-bedroom flat would allow them to share a flat but still to have their own bedrooms.

The two or even three-bedroom unit also responds to the very real need to allow the opportunity of carers with elderly dependents to live with and care for their relatives or friends within a supportive environment.

Research in the United Kingdom confirms that in the private sector, two-bedroom units tend to sell more quickly than one-bedroom units, even though their price is higher. The same research suggests that three-bedroom units could also be justified in certain market conditions[17].

Typical layout for two-bedroom apartment.

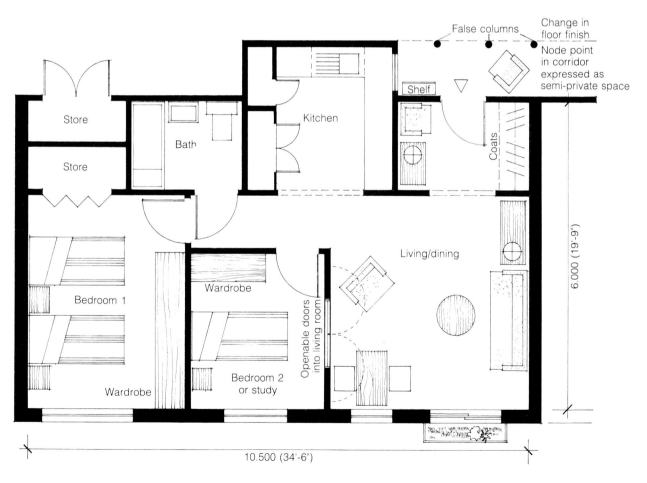

The second bedroom also allows for overnight stays by guests and can double as a study/den/hobby room. The increase in the amount of space for storage and keeping a resident's existing furniture is another advantage of the two-bed unit.

The two-bedroom unit will therefore offer the most flexible arrangement both for potential resident and for developer. However, the inclusion of some one-bedroom and even three-bedroom units should be considered, to extend as far as possible the market range of a development. The exact unit mix for any scheme will, however, need to take account of the anticipated market trends appropriate to its particular area.

Design criteria
—   The one or two- bedroom units add a further layer of complexities and possibilities to planning out the space. Over the years there have emerged recognisable generic groups of plans which, essentially, represent various ways of dealing with the two major planning issues of multi-dwelling design, which are that:
—   Most dwellings will have to be single aspect.
—   The width and depth of each unit and the cost of its repeat value is very much constrained by budget, as well as by site limitations.

Corridor

Store

Space for wardrobe

Bath

Kitchen

Larder unit

Bedroom

Living/dining

5.400

7.800

There is, however, a potential problem in that furniture may have to be placed against the connecting doors if there is not enough wall space provided in the bedroom.

Every available square foot of wall is used at Manston Court, especially in the bedroom, to allow residents to keep their own furniture and personal effects. Note the Teasmade by the bedside table (architects: City of Southampton, Architects Department).

A typical living room at Toldene Court, Croydon, UK, affectionately decorated with personal furniture and memorabilia. Note the television beside the window. Although this position can lead to problems with glare, it appears to be the most favoured one, as the resident can both look out of the window and watch the television from the same chair (architects: the Architects and Building Group, Department of Education & Science).

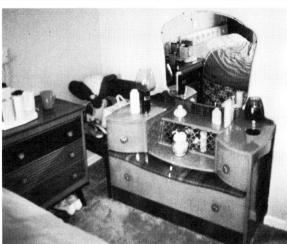

Planning the unit

Peter Phippen, whose practice has had particular experience in developing plan arrangements and has benefited from successive projects, each standing on the shoulders of the last, has said:

We try to make the layout of the flat as flexible as possible. One of the problems is that one can too easily totally predetermine furniture arrangements rather than allow for the possibility of various options to suit individual nees. Peter Phippen.

Phippen Randall and Parkes's proposed layout for a one-bedroom flat for a scheme in Daventry, England, for the United Kingdom Housing Trust clearly illustrates good planning concepts which should apply to all dwelling types.

— The layout is based upon the wide frontage plan, in which the living room occupies approximately two-thirds of the frontage and the bedroom the remaining third. This is because this plan produces good lighting to the living room.

— The layout provides for a dining table and a sitting area against a window, so whatever the activities of the residents, they can enjoy a direct view of the outside.

— The kitchen is then placed inboard, but is open plan with a window onto the corridor, giving a second aspect, looking out onto that space. Apart from providing a view out for the person in the kitchen, such windows have two other functions: they can provide a discreet observation point for the warden and a further outlet for individual self-expression in the corridor, as curtains or items for display can be put in the window.

— The kitchen is planned so that the sink is under the fixed window to the corridor. The oven and base units are positioned together, and there is a short wall so that they are not in full view from the living and dining area.

— The entrance is recessed to define it from the corridor and to accommodate the meter store. An additional store belonging to the residents is provided in the corridor. This leaves the interior of the unit free from another set of doors, but provides a much needed space for residents.

— Between the bedroom and the living room a pair of doors is provided, so that if anyone is confined to bed the doors can be opened to let them remain in contact with the rest of the unit and their partner or visitor during this period.

— Along one side of the kitchen a range of full height built-in cupboards with full height doors have been provided. These are very popular, because items may be stored at preferred level, that is, not at base unit or wall unit height level.

— In the bedroom there is room for residents to bring their own wardrobe.

— The square-shaped living room appears to be the most suitable for furniture arrangements.

— Sufficient space has also been allowed, min. 500mm (1 ft 8 in) for making the bed or beds.

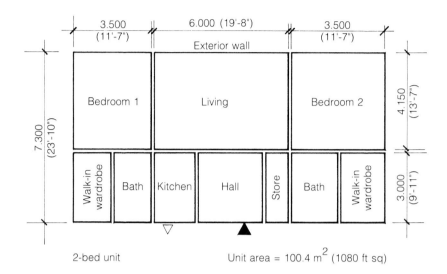

3.500 (11'-7") 6.000 (19'-8") 3.500 (11'-7")

Exterior wall

Bedroom 1 Living Bedroom 2

4.150 (13'-7")

7.300 (23'-10")

Walk-in wardrobe | Bath | Kitchen | Hall | Store | Bath | Walk-in wardrobe

3.000 (9'-11")

2-bed unit

Unit area = 100.4 m^2 (1080 ft sq)

Types of two-bedroom apartment

— Wide frontage necessitated by having to provide daylight to both bedrooms and living room.
— Kitchen planned off living room which can look out onto corridor but separated from living area by circulation path to bedroom.
— Each bedroom has its own bath/WC and store but these can only be reached through the bedroom.
— Plan allows for one or both bedrooms to open off living area.

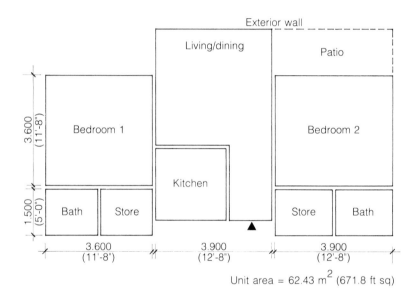

Exterior wall

Living/dining Patio

Bedroom 1 Bedroom 2

3.600 (11'-8")

Kitchen

Bath | Store Store | Bath

1.500 (5'-0")

3.600 (11'-8") 3.900 (12'-8") 3.900 (12'-8")

Unit area = 62.43 m^2 (671.8 ft sq)

Variation on the same theme but with the living/dining space pushed forward, creating the opportunity to provide balconies.

— Two-bedroom unit with one bath/WC.
— Plan allows for bedroom two to open into living room.
— Both kitchen and bathroom reached from circulation route.

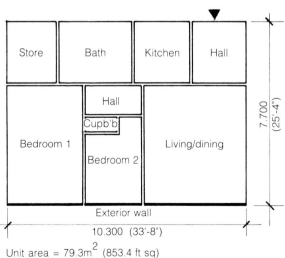

Store | Bath | Kitchen | Hall

Hall

Cupb'b

Bedroom 1 Bedroom 2 Living/dining

7.700 (25'-4")

Exterior wall

10.300 (33'-8")

Unit area = 79.3m^2 (853.4 ft sq)

Further design criteria for individual kitchen and bathrooms within dwellings

As with all types of housing, the design and hardware of the kitchen and bathroom are what draws most comments from users. Considering the size of the market, it is somewhat surprising that hardware for kitchens and bathrooms for elderly people does not figure more prominently in the domestic fittings market. Both kitchen and bathroom will need a common attention to detail, in particular to the ability of an arthritic hand to grip a tap and to turn it on, or to open a cupboard, drawer or window.

Also, the use of contrasting colour and texture should be brought through into the design of both kitchen and bathroom. White sanitaryware against white tiles with white walls will aggravate any difficulty in distinguishing features and are therefore potentially hazardous. In the kitchen the worktop should be distinguished by colour from the wall unit, tiled splashback and so on.

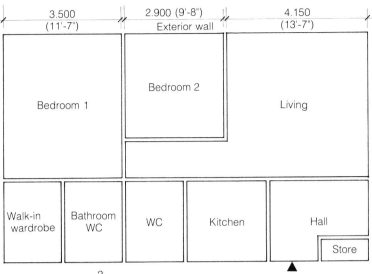

Unit area = 69.66 m^2 (749.5 ft sq)

— A second
bedroom or den
with a slightly nar-
rower frontage.
— The plan
allows for WC to
be accessed from
hall.
— Kitchen sepa-
rated from living
area by circu-
lation path.

Of course further possibilities open up on small, clustered plan arrangements on high rise projects	where each unit may enjoy either a double or even triple aspect. (Unit layout at Wilson Park, Penn-	sylvania USA (architects: Jordan Mitchell Inc., in association with Wallace Roberts and Todd).

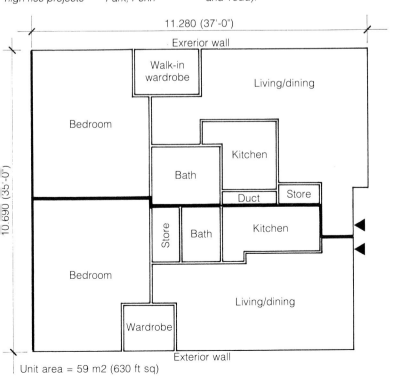

Unit area = 59 m2 (630 ft sq)

Kitchen design

The principles of good domestic kitchen design apply equally to kitchens for elderly people. However, certain criteria should be reconsidered and the convenience, safety and efficiency of the layout be addressed. A particular problem noted in many existing schemes is that storage is often inadequate and inaccessible.

In a study conducted at the Massachusetts Institute of Technology (MIT) it was found that many residents voiced concern regarding the insufficient space in the kitchen to store basic items such as pots, pans, utensils and appliances. The need for more working counter space was also voiced.

Sometimes traditional use patterns need to be modified to meet changing requirements, of which people may be unaware. Single seating space at sink level is recommended for elderly or handicapped. Space for storage of sink-orientated materials should be provided within easy reach, but perhaps not directly underneath the sink[17].

Comments regarding kitchen sizes are perhaps another indication of the time-lag in terms of user requirements in housing for elderly people. Because of budget constraints, kitchens have always been planned to a minimum. This may have suited the first generations of residents in sheltered housing, as the kitchens they may have left, particularly in the publicly funded sector, may not have been much larger. However, as the population of residents begins increasingly to include those who have been used to larger, well-equipped kitchens, user expectations of more space will grow.

Kitchen appliances (dishwashers, washing machines, tumble dryers, freezers, microwave ovens) while not expected in the homes of our current elderly, will therefore no doubt increasingly be perceived as a legitimate requirement by future generations of elderly people, particularly in the private sector.

It is important to remember that the kitchen may well still be seen by residents as the centre of their home, so this important base from which to enact the role of the mother/wife should, as far as possible, be allowed to remain a part of the new environment.

Design criteria
The design should allow for a possible reduction in residents' mobility and dexterity.
— Provision should be made for a person to sit at the sink and at the worktop, so that they can prepare food and carry out basic kitchen chores without having to stand.
— Where there are openable windows in the kitchen, they should not be on the far side of a worktop, which would make it difficult to reach across and open them.

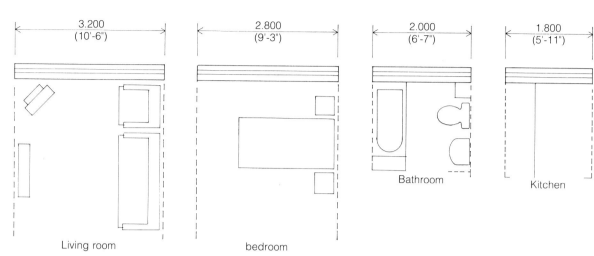

Minimum widths in planning the dwelling unit. Bathrooms and kitchens may be planned 'inboard'. Dimensions are minimum and not necessarily preferred, but may be applied when assessing existing building shells.

Living room   bedroom   Bathroom   Kitchen

3.200 (10'-6")   2.800 (9'-3")   2.000 (6'-7")   1.800 (5'-11")

Low level storage can make access difficult.

— Allowance should be made for the range of additional appliances discussed above, as they will become a preferred user requirement of future elderly residents. It should also be noted that residents may prefer to bring their own appliances for use in their new kitchen.

— Although worktop widths of 500mm (1 ft 8 in) and a height of 850mm (2 ft 9½ in) are generally recommended, this does not necessarily fit the majority of under-worktop kitchen appliances, which are designed for use with 600mm (2 ft) wide and 860mm (2 ft 10 in) minimum, or in some cases 900mm (3 ft). Worktop heights of 860mm (2 ft 10 in), with widths of 600mm (2 ft) may be required. Standard worktop heights and widths therefore may need to be reconsidered.

— The ability to eat in the kitchen, say for light snacks or breakfast, is also important, so a breakfast bar should be incorporated (height approximately 760mm (30½ in)).

— Sinks should be deep enough, i.e. 150mm (6 in) minimum to allow for some clothes washing by hand.

At Toldene Court, Croydon, UK, the sink area has space underneath for a stool to allow a resident to sit. Note the lever taps and long-reach tap spout (architects: the Architects' and Building Group, Department of Education and Science).

— The kitchen layout should be a U or L shape rather than a single line one, to minimise walking distance.

— Where kitchens are internally planned, ventilation will require careful study to ensure that cooking smells or steam are quickly vented outside the dwelling. The ventilation system should not have to rely upon a resident switching a ventilator on or off, as this may not be done if that resident is anxious about using too much electricity.

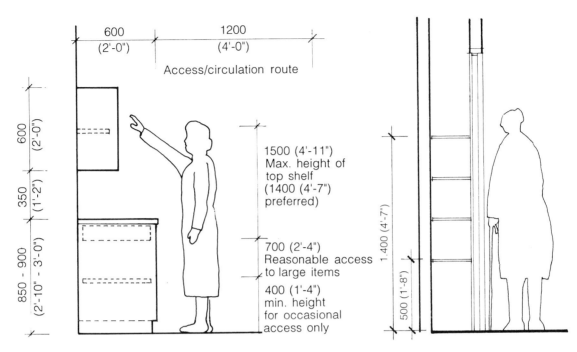

600 (2'-0")   1200 (4'-0")

Access/circulation route

600 (2'-0")

350 (1'-2")

850 - 900 (2'-10" - 3'-0")

1500 (4'-11")
Max. height of
top shelf
(1400 (4'-7")
preferred)

700 (2'-4")
Reasonable access
to large items

400 (1'-4")
min. height
for occasional
access only

1.400 (4'-7")

500 (1'-8")

Key dimensions for kitchen unit working heights.

To overcome some of the difficulties that have been experienced in having to reach up to wall units, open shelves do the work of to a larder and have proved very popular in several projects. The shelves can easily be enclosed by two simple doors.

The highest shelf in a wall unit should be no higher than 1500mm (4 ft 11 in).

Opening a window can become a problem when it is positioned over a unit which projects 600mm (2 ft).

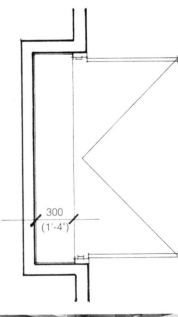

300 (1'-4")

Bathroom design

Activity

In order to preserve independence for as long as possible, the design of the bathroom is critical. Peter Phippen.

Being able to use one's own bathroom and toilet without assistance or having to surrender to outside help are the areas of activity which, more than any other, represent that subtle threshold of change from independent living to institutional care. As with many of the other features of housing for elderly people, therefore, the quality and design of the hardware can help save that threshold from being crossed prematurely.

One of the design issues regarding bathrooms has been whether or not to provide a shower. It may be provided on the assumption that elderly residents find the use of a shower easier than having to step in or out of a bath, and where space permits, a walk-in shower in addition to a bath would certainly offer more flexibility. However, to provide showers as an alternative to baths would be to restrict an individual's choice of washing. There is no evidence to support claims that showers are more convenient or safer to use than baths.

The fear of slipping in the bath or of being unable to get out of it is understandable. To help in manoeuvrability, grab-rails are often fitted. However, because the degree of assistance

Plan and sections of bathroom layout for individual dwellings showing possible positions of grab rails (subject to individual needs).

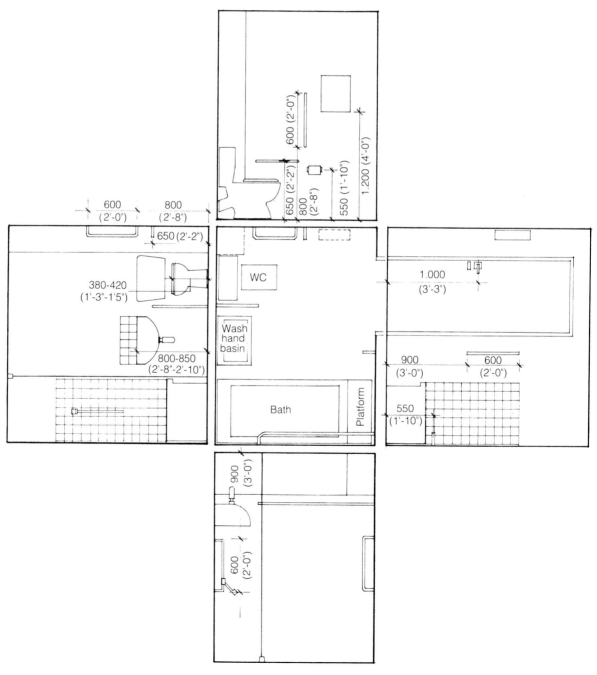

Cruciform tap handles are a more subtle choice for an easily usable tap, as opposed to the lever action taps.

Resident's bathroom at Fullwell Court, Milton Keynes, UK, with grab rail. Note the cruciform taps and non-slip surface for the bath (architects: The Tooley and Foster Partnership).

required will vary from resident to resident, many housing managers believe that the grab-rails should be individually fitted, to match each resident's particular need.

If a grab-rail is fitted just inches too high or too low, at best it will become a nuisance and cause frustration and at worst it will become a potential source of danger. Pauline O'Driscoll.

Residents who begin their retirement years active may not want to see a bathroom cluttered with rails and poles. It may cause offence, implying the need for premature assistance.

We build-in very few physical features that assist in living from day one. Instead, we prefer to customize the unit to the individual rather than install fittings that can be symbol of certain frailty. R. Stephan.

However, as assistance is required, the appropriate type and size of aid can be fitted to match precise individual requirements.

Linen storage. Minimum and maximum heights for storage shelves.

Design criteria
— Doors to bathrooms should open outwards and be fitted with locks that can be opened from the outside. This is in case a resident collapses inside the bathroom and obstructs the door. Alternatively, a sliding door arrangement may be acceptable in some cases, although again this is not considered a conventional, domestic living pattern.
— The bath itself should be flat-bottomed with a ribbed and non-slip base. A maximum length of 1550mm (5 ft 1 in) is recommended to prevent the chance of slipping down and becoming totally immersed. The width should be as wide as possible, say, 800mm (2 ft 7½ in) to allow for greater manoeuvrability. The rim height of the bath should be at a maximum of 450mm (1 ft 6 in). This is to allow easier access to the bath.
— The WC should have a toilet seat height of 450mm (1 ft 6 in). The lever handle of the cistern should be at 1000mm (3ft).
— The washhand basin should be fixed

securely to the wall to withstand the person's full weight, and should have a rim height of 800–850mm (2 ft 7½in–2 ft 10½in).
— Where grab rails and support rails are provided, they should have non-slip surfaces, such as ribbed pvc.
— A bath platform should be provided to help the transfer into a bath, from either a wheelchair or a standing position.

Storage

The ability to store personal items is a test of how well the design of the unit allows for residents to identify with their new surroundings by bringing with them furniture, appliances or simply mementoes from their past. The problems of storage can be aggravated by an increasing disability to reach up or down to retrieve stored items from a cupboard[18]. The need to provide adequate stor-

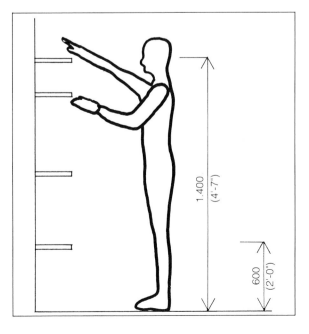

age is, therefore, just as important as in any apartment design.

Four categories of storage may be identified:

— Clothes storage

It should be assumed that in most cases adequate space must be provided in the bedroom area for at least one double wardrobe, for even if the unit is for a single person the resident may may wish to bring with him/her a double wardrobe from the previous home. The building-in of wardrobe units can of course be more space-efficient, but this has to be balanced against the advantages of allowing a resident to bring their own furniture (see chapter 3).

— Linen storage

This can be built-in, but care should be taken to ensure that the shelves are no lower than 600mm (2 ft) and no higher than 1400mm (4 ft 7 in) to ensure accessibility. If shelves are too deep (more than 600mm (2 ft) this may also cause difficulties in reaching the rear of the shelf. As with any linen store they should be situated off a circulation area, and should be well vented and heated.

— Broom cupboard

Whilst it is questionable as to how useful a broom cupboard will be for the very frail resident who will

be unable to clean for him/her self, the provision of a broom cupboard should still be considered, as it may still be used by home helps who clean the dwellings. For the residents still able to use a vacuum cleaner, a broom cupboard is of course an essential (although sometimes forgotten) item.

— General storage

A common complaint about any apartment design is a lack of general storage for miscellaneous items such as suitcases and trunks. Housing for the elderly is no exception. However, because of possible limited mobility, deep narrow stores would be of limited use. An associated problem of providing stores within a dwelling is that they take up wall space which would be valuable for other items of furniture. Phippen Randall and Parkes's plan in their scheme at Wokingham overcame this by placing the general store outside the dwelling.

Balconies

Many luxury apartments may include a balcony off both living and bedroom areas, or for ground floor apartments a patio. Such spaces do offer private external space. Balconies would appear a desirable feature for housing for elderly people. The provision of easily accessible external space would particularly benefit frail elderly who may become building-bound. However, the additional cost of a balcony and whether it would mean sacrificing interior dwelling space should be carefully considered. In high rise developments balconies may prove a potential source of anxiety and danger and should perhaps be at least semi-enclosed as a conservatory.

Patio areas at ground floor may also pose additional problems of security. It is therefore essential that any external space is perceived by both resident and passer-by as private and defensible space.

Reception counter for house manager at Golda Meir House, Newton, Mass. USA (architects: Larkin Glassman and Prager).

Layout of office and reception counter at Covenant House, Brighton, Mass. USA (architects: Larkin Glassman and Prager).

Warden's office at Fullwell Court, Milton Keynes, UK (architects: The Tooley and Forster Partnership). The Warden's primary role is to act as good neighbour to residents.

Areas for Use by Staff

The ability to service residents' needs, especially those in extra care, will depend on the type of facilities provided on site for staff in administration, nursing/medical and maintenance/cleaning functions.

Administration

If the development is large enough, there will be a need for adequate provision for staff dealing with the business administration of the building.

The warden or house manager

Activity

In many respects the warden or house manager can become a focal point for the residents, fulfilling a multitude of roles which will vary according to the management policy of a particular development and, to some degree, the personality of those involved. Traditionally, the warden has been looked upon as a good neighbour, maintaining a very high degree of informal personal contact.

However, as developments' populations age, so demands upon the warden can grow; in some cases beyond the physical capacity or professional training of one individual. It is therefore important to ensure that the warden's services are planned in the context of a team of managers and, if necessary, personal care and nursing staff, to provide full support when required[19]. In the United Kingdom, most sheltered housing developments include on-site living accommodation for a resident warden and, depending on the size of the development, this may also include accommodation for a deputy warden. The aim is to provide 24-hour cover. However, organisations such as Help the Aged are now considering 24-hour cover by wardens/managers working on shift, which resembles the arrangement for nursing cover. John White of Help the Aged sees that rather than just provide warden accommodation, all types of housing developments for elderly people should be supported by what he calls a service centre: that is, a system which will offer:
— *An office space* for service providers, including professionals from the local health authorities.
— *A 24 hour emergency cover team* linked into emergency call systems.
— *A day care centre.*
— *Relief and respite* care beds.
— *An information and advisory bureau* to cover such areas as financial and welfare rights,

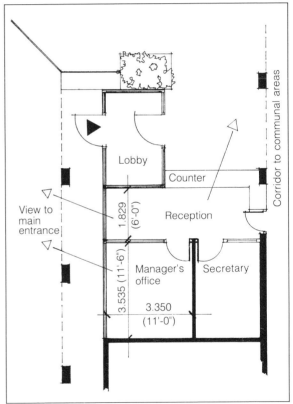

To provide a greater flexibility in use, consultation rooms/doctors' offices should be planned to accommodate a variety of functions.

building and structural repair and ground maintenance.

Design criteria
— To promote a more informal threshold between the warden/manager and the resident, a reception desk overlooking the main entrance should be considered. This can often allow a more spontaneous exchange than a mere office would. However, linked to the reception desk should also be an office in which confidential conversations may take place. This space would normally hold a desk, some space for filing and a small table.

Nursing and medical facilities

Because of the exacting needs of any medical facility, it is always advisable that the designer should listen to the medical staff who will use the facility, and develop a brief in close association with the medical planning adviser of the funding or client body.

Consulting room/doctor's office

Because residents will not always be able to visit their family doctor, in schemes containing over 60 units consideration should be given to providing rooms with the same type of basic facilities as a doctor's office, in which visiting medical staff may consult, examine or treat residents. The number of rooms would depend largely on the location and scale of the development, but a minimum provision would be one consulting room per 60 residents.

In large scale life care communities, the medical facilities can operate as a health centre, with its own reception and waiting area. To optimise use of space, the consulting rooms should be usable for a variety of health care functions. A room of approximately 11m² (120 sq ft) should answer most requirements. These rooms should be on the ground floor, easily accessible to all residents and to visiting medical staff.

Nurse's base office

Associated with any medical rooms there should also be an office of at least 11m² (120 sq ft) for any nursing or care staff who may have to carry out administrative duties and store records in a confidential and secure space. The size of this office again will depend upon the anticipated number of permanent medical staff.

Utility rooms

Utility rooms serving both the medical facility and residents' dwellings will be required, to accommodate the following functions:
— *Clean utility* for storage of equipment, drugs

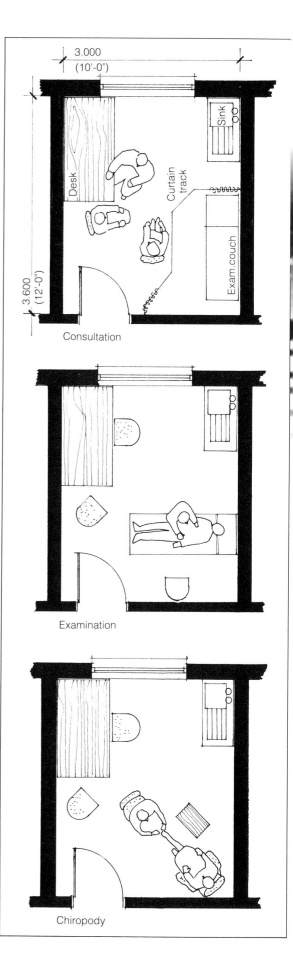

Consultation

Examination

Chiropody

At Fullwell Court, Milton Keynes, UK, the policy of extra care as developed by The Anchor Housing Association includes for a base from which care staff may carry out their administrative duties and store any records (architects: The Tooley and Foster Partnership).

Nurse base at Waverly Heights, Gladwyne, Pennsylvania USA. Larger scale developments such as the life care community at Waverly Heights has its own health care facility with 37 nursing and personal care beds. The nursing and residential care facilities were planned with the client/nursing representatives acting as full members of the design team to achieve the planned facilities required (architects: Sullivan Associates).

Staff facilities

Depending upon the number of staff employed, there should be adequate provision for staff rest rooms, in which coffee breaks and light meals may be taken. Staff showers and WCs should also be included. Special facilities for kitchen staff will also need to comply with local codes and regulations.

General storage

A cleaning store room to include a cleaner's sink and cupboards for storing cleaning equipment should be located on each floor.
— While bed linen may either be handled individually by residents or centrally, provision should still be made for a central linen store near the laundry, with satellite linen stores on each floor. This is to ensure easy access to residents' bedrooms.

The need for these facilities may, of course, not immediately apply in those developments where younger or more active elderly are accommodated. However, as a development population ages and becomes more frail, demand for the level of service will inevitably increase. Consideration should therefore be given to the possibility of providing an extra care base, from which such services could be delivered in the future, even if extra care is not operational from day one. For example, allowance should be made at design stage for a ground floor apartment to be convertible for use as a base, or for a planned extension to a facility when required. Such foresight will help to ensure that the development will be able to accommodate the changing needs of its residents, and will not force a resident to leave prematurely what they may have hoped would be their last home.

and for the testing and storing of samples, e.g. blood and urine. The storage of drugs will need to comply with any local codes/regulations. This may be planned adjacent to a speciment WC. The clean utility room may be adjacent to the nurse base/office.
— *Dirty utility/sluice room* for the cleaning of soiled bed linen, emptying of bed pans etc. This should be within easy reach of the dwellings. At least one utility room per floor or wing of any development should be provided.

Clean and dirty utility rooms based upon layout by Geoffrey Salmon of Salmon Speed Architects.

Dirty utility
1 Macerator
2 Sluices and sink
3 Shelving

Clean utility (right)
1 Base storage units
2 Shelving or wall storage units (to include lockable drugs cupboard)
3 Stainless steel sink and drawer
4 Waste bins

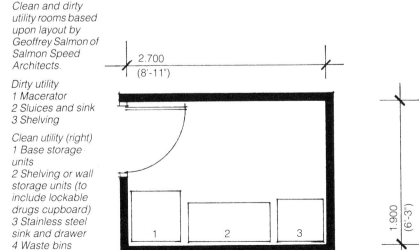

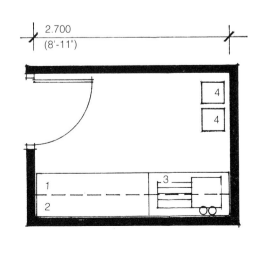

Key dimensions (minimum) for parking spaces for semi-ambulant person.

Key dimensions (minimum) for parking space for wheelchair user.

External Spaces

Car parking

There is a lower car ownership among the elderly than among the rest of the adult population. The increase in car ownership amongst the current middle-aged population will eventually filter through to the next generation of elderly and result in more people entering old age as car owners. However, whilst younger active elderly may bring their own cars with them to their new home, there will be factors affecting the length of time the residents will be able to retain their cars. These are:

— Financial considerations, as the car becomes a liability in terms of running costs.

— The advent of illness or any disability may leave a resident unable to drive.

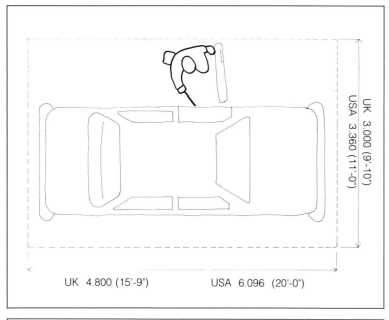

UK 4.800 (15'-9")   USA 6.096 (20'-0")

UK 3.000 (9'-10")
USA 3.360 (11'-0")

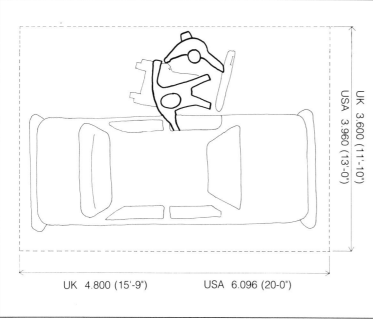

UK 4.800 (15'-9")   USA 6.096 (20-0")

UK 3.600 (11'-10")
USA 3.960 (13'-0")

— In the United Kingdom, drivers aged 70 years and over must renew their licence every three years subject to declaration of fitness. If a doctor's report is required by an insurance company this can, lead to a person's licence being withdrawn.

— Residents may choose to stop driving, especially if the site is well located for shopping and transport facilities.

— A spouse who is the only driver of the partnership may die.

Accordingly, it can be assumed that the car ownership of a resident population may well decline over time, due to the above factors.

Nonetheless, as a population of residents does age, there may be more visitors to the site; friends or relatives may now visit more often to compensate for the resident not being able to leave their home as frequently as before. There will also be an increase in the number of service support staff (e.g. doctors, meals-on-wheels, personal care staff, nursing staff).

Car parking provision, therefore calls for flexible and realistic consideration, both by developers and by local planning officers. Each site must be treated individually. The dogma of applying inflexible dwelling-to-car-space ratios can too often result in totally inappropriate car parking provision, and the actual provision of car spaces will need to be assessed in relation to each scheme and to the type of resident to be accommodated.

Baker and Parry have recommended the following standards which will be a useful guide, subject to the initial consultations and negotiations with local planning/traffic officers[20].

Type of accommodation	Ratio of car space to dwelling
For one-bedroom town centre schemes for older elderly.	1:4
Two-bedroom accommodation or out of town locations.	1:2
As above, but with anticipated high proportion of younger elderly, i.e. 55 plus.	1:1

— The design and layout of a car park should allow the shortest possible distance between the resident's parking space and their dwelling.

— Determination of lighting levels in the car park should bear in mind frail elderly passengers being taken to and from a parked car: see p. 75 on the need to provide an adequate entrance canopy.

— Wheelchair users and disabled elderly may still drive their own cars. Wider parking bays should be provided and be clearly marked for exclusive use for disabled drivers. A minimum of one disabled user's car space per 15 dwellings should be allowed.

— Where covered car spaces are to be provided, it should be noted that carports are pre-

Raised planting beds allow residents to tend to plants without having to bend down.

ferred to garages, as they can offer greater flexibility for manoeuvring[21].
— Some adapted cars (those for handicapped users) may require electrical charging points by their car space.

Landscape

Depending upon each site's location, the potential for providing well designed spaces around any development should be investigated as an integral part of the whole scheme.
Because the costs of maintaining the external areas will affect the overall service charges, it will be important to design a landscape that will require minimum maintenance.
The choice and location of planting should take account of the following factors:
— The arrangement of any planting scheme will form part of that all-important view out.
— As much variety and 'activity' as possible should be designed into the scheme: plants that change with the seasons, that move with the wind and have a variety of colour, and which attract birds and butterflies.
— Such planting should not be too far from vantage points in the building, bearing in mind possible failing eyesight amongst many of the residents.

External sitting areas

The chance to sit out in a protected and sheltered space during fine weather will be an important

design feature, However, many residents will not wish to wander too far from the building.
— They will want to keep within a short distance of any toilets.
— They may not wish to be out of sight of care staff.
— They may be physically unable to travel too far.
The external seating areas should therefore be immediately adjacent either to the communal lounge area/or dining area, or be related to private dwellings.

750
(2'-6")

The conservatory at Claverton Court leads out to a communal sitting area to provide a protected and secure space for residents, defined by the landscape itself (photo: Judy Cass).

At Claverton Court, Chester, UK, the use of conservatory spaces to both ground and first floors allows for residents to sit in a semi external environment throughout the year where they may sit out as well as be able to tend their plants (photo: John Mills). (Architects: Brock Carmichael Associates, and BCA Landscape).

Waverly Heights, USA: a green-house in the garden is a simple yet often overlooked addition to any shared-use facility (photo Jim Schafer).

Where lounge or dining spaces are provided, they should be able to open out to paved external areas, where the activities of dining or just sitting may extend into an external space during fine weather. Conservatories can often provide a semi-external environment which can be used throughout the year. Where dwellings are on the ground floor, both bedroom and living area should have some opening onto a small private external area to be enjoyed as an extension of the private living space.

However, in designing the landscape of these spaces the following should be noted:

— Security and privacy, especially in the private external areas, must be maintained. The area must be protected against misuse or intrusion by non-residents. If residents feel at all anxious about the security of a communal open space, they may not use it. If there is any anxiety about a private external space next to a dwelling, this could distress its inhabitants and make the scheme less attractive to potential residents. Adequate screening and fencing must therefore be provided.

— Although some residents will have moved to a housing scheme so as not to have the burden of maintaining a garden, many may still enjoy the chance to grow plants and keep a small planting area. Raised planting beds not lower than 750mm (2 ft 6 in) should be provided to allow residents the choice of some form of limited gardening.

Environmental Hardware and Services

The process of ageing brings into focus four critical factors affecting environmental comfort: manipulation (the ability to operate the various items of hardware most of us would normally take for granted), heating, lighting and sound.

Manipulation

Windows: Apart from satisfying the basic criteria of window design, which should apply to any building type, *all* windows should be designed so that they are:
— Easy to clean (either by residents or staff).
— Draught-proof.
— Large enough to allow views out where appropriate and to satisfy the daylight require-ments of the various room functions.
— Easily opened and closed and with good control of the amount of opening required[1].

Doors: Basic criteria for doors are:
— They should be wide enough to allow easy passage for wheelchair users or those residents who may use a walking frame. Minimum clear opening width 775mm (2ft 6in).
— They may be easily opened and closed. If self-closing devices are required by fire codes, then consideration should be given to door closers which act only in the event of a fire warn-ing. Heavily sprung doors should be avoided.
— Entrance doors to flat should incorporate a clear toughened glass panel to allow residents to see callers. Peep-holes can be a problem, in that it can be difficult for the height adjustment to suit each resident. They can also prove hard to use for residents with failing eyesight.
— They should be easily distinguished from the rest of the wall fabric.
— As previously discussed in chapter 3, failing eyesight can lead to difficulty in perceiving changes in texture or contrast. A contrasting colour on the door frame is sometimes used to emphasise the position of the door.

Ironmongery

It should be possible to clearly see, reach and then easily grip a cupboard, window or a door handle: that is the basic criterion for all iron-mongery. For doors, lever handles which can be easily distinguished from the door itself should be set at 1000mm (3 ft 3in) above finished floor level.

Door ironmongery and light switches do not normally present problems if they are set low at 1000mm (3 ft 3 in) above finished floor level for chair-bound users, and if they are selected with arthritic fingers in mind. Peter Phippen.

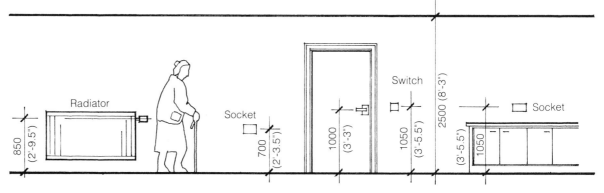

An electric glo-fire can act as a safe and convenient alternative to the traditional coal fire as a focal point of a living room.

Some systems provide for the warden to remain in contact with all residents whilst out of the office by switching into a localised control.

Service outlets

Service outlets should again be positioned bearing in mind the mobility restrictions of the people who are going to use them. The recommended heights for electrical socket outlets vary from 700mm (2 ft 3½ in) to 1000mm (3 ft 3 in) above finished floor level with socket outlets in the kitchen being set at 1150mm (3 ft 9 in). It is sometimes also recommended that the design of the outlet should place the two switches at opposite ends of the outlet.

Light switches should be placed at a height of

between 900mm (3 ft) and 1050mm (3 ft 5½ in). Being able to see and locate the light switch is of importance, and consideration should be given to the use of the coloured fittings that are now becoming available instead of plain white ones. To facilitate distinguishing between a light switch and a socket outlet, it would be of help to locate the socket outlet at, say 700mm (2 ft 3½ in) and the light switch at 1150mm (3 ft 9 in). The use of a different colour for each would also help to distinguish them.

Heating

I don't think that there is anything more abused and more important than adequate heating in the design of facilities for older people. Of course there will be a whole range of different comfort levels amongst residents in relation to their age and physical condition. However, there will be a much higher temperature need. It is not only the temperature itself, but also the designing out of any draughts that will be important. Joe Jordan.

The actual method of heating will largely depend upon the location, the available sources of energy and the scale and design layout of a particular scheme.

Whatever form of heating is to be chosen, the following factors should be borne in mind:
— As residents become older their ability to retain their own body heat will lessen, and they will feel the cold more.
— For circulation areas a minimum background heating of 18°C (65°F) should be maintained. However, for individual dwellings a universal comfort temperature cannot be determined, as some will of course feel the cold more than others. As a general guide in the UK though, the heating should be designed to provide an even temperature of 21°C (70°F) throughout the dwelling when the outside temperature is −1°C (30°F). This would also apply to the communal areas and shared facilities.

Minimum maintained temperature levels.

Radiator thermostat control, easily operated at a height of 850mm (2 ft 9½ in).

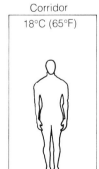

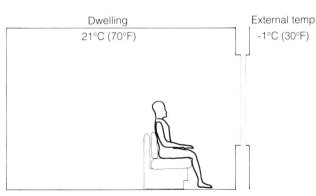

Corridor	Dwelling	External temp
18°C (65°F)	21°C (70°F)	-1°C (30°F)

Computerised monitor and communication system by Tunstall Telecom, UK, allows for centralised monitoring of residents, within the development and of other developments and individuals, locally or further afield: as used at Oakfield Lodge, Redbridge, England (architects: London Borough of Redbridge).

Combined pull-cord and speech call system allowing two way communication between resident and warden/house manager.

— It is important to allow residents to adjust the temperature easily in their own dwellings. There can be problems with total control, in that some residents, for fear of paying high heating bills, will deliberately turn their heating too low or right off, thereby endangering their health. This, turn, implies a responsibility on management to keep a watch for this. A compromise is perhaps to consider a control over the temperature range, or a thermomatic device which would provide a basic level of heat, and could then be individually boosted if required. Consideration should be given to providing low temperature sensors, to alert staff in the event of a local heating failure.

— Heating appliances should be safe to use, touch and control. Bearing in mind mental frailty, fires using combustible fuel such as coal, gas and oil could be potentially lethal.

— Nevertheless the heat source should be visible and recognisable. Concealed heating, while no doubt able to provide the level of heat required, may not satisfy a resident's desire to sit close to and be comforted by an identifiable heat source. Apart from the television, the traditional focal point of a living room tends in UK to be the fireplace. Coal fires are not recommended, but some source of heat which can fulfil the same function should be considered, such as an electric Glo-coal fire (with flickering internal light) which may not provide all the heat to a dwelling, but is nonetheless a safe alternative to a coal fire.

Doors, handles, stairs and nosings all clearly defined by contrasting use of colour. Rosewood Square, London, England. (Architects: London Borough of Hammersmith).

— The avoidance of draughts is a basic design criteria for any housing scheme. For elderly people this requirement is even more critical. This being so, heating systems which rely upon warm air being circulated throughout the dwellings are not recommended, as all air movement is likely to be perceived as a draught. Respiratory problems can also be aggravated by warm air systems.

— In warmer climates, excessive heat and solar gain during hot summers can also cause severe discomfort, especially for residents unable to venture out. Air cooling and air conditioning should, in these cases, be incorporated.

— Where heating pipes or radiators are exposed, care should be taken to avoid the danger of scalding. Radiators should therefore be clearly defined visually.

Lighting

Good lighting helps avoid confusion. A lot of problems connected with confusion happen with illusions. People see something and may misinterpret it. Dr Anne Roberts

The need to be able to see clearly, and to distinguish objects, services, signs, clocks, noticeboards and changes of level is important. This is particularly important because of the increased danger of fails. In the daytime windows and interior surface treatments should aim to minimize glare and silhouetting. For artificial lighting overall lighting will tend to flatten surfaces. Instead, a combination of general and localised task lighting would enable features such as signs, doors, steps and changes of level to be picked out clearly. It is not only a matter of the intensity of light provided, but rather of its ability to emphasise contrast. Right use of colour will enhance contrast. The colour of doors, ironmongery, switches, and signs should make them easily distinguishable from their surrounding surfaces. Because signs cannot always be read from a distance, they should ideally be placed at eye-level so that closer inspection is possible.

Sound

As their hearing deteriorates, residents may have to talk louder to be heard or may increase the volume of a television or radio. The overall result can be that sound levels are quite high, in both communal areas and dwellings: the image of these developments as inhabited by quiet old ladies is misleading. While the current generation of elderly tend not to use hi-fi equipment it will no doubt become a common feature for future generations. All this implies careful attention to the acoustic design of the fabric of the building.

There is a need to develop a higher level of sound insulation between the living spaces in ordinary apartment dwellings. Problems of sound also become critical in the communal areas. The

Construction of dwelling units in regard to transmission of airborne sound.

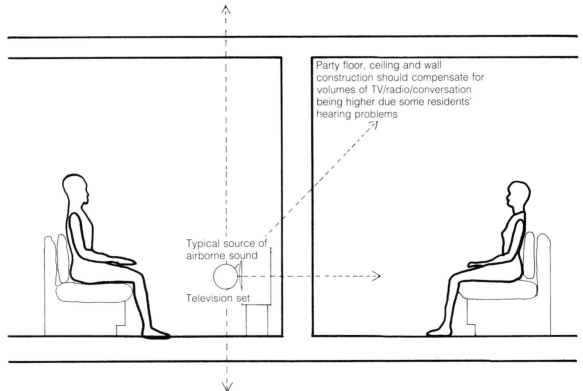

Party floor, ceiling and wall construction should compensate for volumes of TV/radio/conversation being higher due some residents' hearing problems

Typical source of airborne sound

Television set

major interference with elderly people's speech comprehension tends to be in a group situation, where there is simultaneous speech or speech at cross purposes, or any background distraction. There can be a difficulty in deciphering what is being said from the background level of sound. It's therefore important to provide an acoustic environment in which the background level of noise, which might occur particularly in the dining room and lounge areas, is reduced. Joe Jordan

Alarm and communication systems

The impact of new technology is also having its effect on housing for elderly people.

Numerous and diverse alarm systems are appearing on the market, each seemingly more sophisticated and offering more facilities. This field will no doubt continue to grow and develop. Any alarm and call system chosen should fulfil the following minimum criteria.
— An emergency alarm system should enable residents to summon assistance from staff on a 24-hour basis.
— The system should link all dwellings plus any communal areas, WCs, bathrooms etc. to a central control.
— The system should be simple to operate and must also be fully maintained and serviced under a management contract.

Methods of activating an alarm

Current systems rely on residents raising an alarm by any or a combination of the following:
— Pulling a cord, which should be located in each room of a dwelling including the bathroom (note: it is in the bathroom that most difficulties or accidents are likely to occur).
— Pressing a pendant that will be worn by the resident, usually around the neck.
— Failing to step on a pressure pad outside the bathroom, i.e. activation of alarm by passive default.

The use of the cord entails the cord reaching down to floor level so that it can be pulled after a fall. However, in practice the cord is often tied up by the resident to avoid its misuse by visiting children or being entangled during cleaning. The positions of the cord can also unnecessarily predetermine the arrangement of furniture in the dwelling. Alarm cords can also be confused with the pullcords for lights to the kitchen or bathroom if sited too near each other. The neck pendant overcomes this, but does rely upon the resident

remembering (or choosing) to wear it. The use of a pendant is perhaps more suited to or more readily accepted by frail residents, as many active elderly may consider its use unnecessary and an intrusion.

Methods of alerting staff

The methods of alerting staff are generally:
— By sounding an alarm bell or siren which is heard either throughout the building or through a bleeper to be worn by staff.
— By the resident being able to talk to staff through the communication system and inform them what is wrong.
— By raising the alarm through a special facility on the resident's telephone.

The alarm bell or siren will need to be noticed immediately by staff. It is perhaps not always appropriate, especially in the case of false alarms, for other residents to hear the siren too. It might be confused with a fire alarm, or in any case could cause anxiety and disturbance, particularly at night. This brings in the question of just what 'an emergency' is. House managers and wardens usually have their stories about the resident who fell out of bed and lay on the floor all night but did not raise the alarm for fear of waking the neighbours, while there are also those residents who have used the alarm merely to ask for a light bulb to be replaced. The most effective method is one by which a resident can first talk direct to a member of staff, because this means:
— Residents can summon help or merely tell staff of a problem and be able to describe it before the staff member takes action.
— As the resident knows that they can first talk to staff before the alarm sets off sirens or bells, the resident will not feel too intimidated to use it.
— The system should also allow the warden or house manager to make and receive calls from and to any part of the building including dwellings, circulation spaces, and of course communal areas.

Many house managers and wardens have stated that whatever system is finally adopted it can never be viewed as an alternative or substitute for regular, personal contact by supervisory staff.

This is particularly critical in the case of residents who become mentally frail. The confused resident may not even recognise the need to alert staff in the event of a real emergency, and in the event, they may well be unable to comprehend the mechanics, however, simple, of any alarm system.

New Directions

In any assessment of future trends and needs it will be important to recognise a general fact about design and buildings. Buildings are expensive to develop and take a long time to build. They are also rarely updated, or modified quickly enough to respond to changing needs. In short, buildings can be prone to an incurable time-lag, in that they do not reflect where we are but rather tell us where we were when they were originally designed.

Buildings both in the United States and the United Kingdom designed to accommodate only active elderly people some ten years ago are now encountering the problems of adapting to a resident population in need of additional support and care in order to maintain an independent life. The provision of a facility which will cope with the changing needs of its resident population throughout their ageing process appears to be the goal towards which many housing managers, public sponsors and private developers are moving.

The integration of facilities for older people into organisations or complexes that will serve the varying needs through the ageing process is certainly a development that we can depend upon happening. There is sufficient evidence in America at present that not only are the number of life care communities now proliferating, but that they are forming from many different directions. Sophisticated development organisations are undertaking projects on a large scale, whilst smaller enterprises are simply adding to their existing facilities to increase their range of accommodation and services. Nursing homes are, for example, adding independent living housing to their schemes and will then, no doubt, be adding to this social day centres to provide a community-based long care facility.

Because the pace of change appears to be accelerating, new actors will come onto the field that we cannot even predict. Joe Jordan.

The method by which the ability to respond to changing needs is achieved appears to be taking two directions. One is the provision of different types of accommodation within sight of each other, so that residents are moved to more suitable accommodation within the framework of a care and support hierarchy: they pass from independent living to nursing care. This segregation of active from frail elderly who may require medical and nursing care is, then, part of the philosophy of life care developments.

The idea is to promote a concept of wellness amongst the population. The medical and service areas are not really meant to be an ever present facility within the day-to-day experience of the building. Andrew Sullivan

The other method is to simply upgrade and increase the level of service input to a resident as and when required. This necessitates the input of services which can monitor and care for residents at dispersed locations. This has the advantage of allowing residents to remain in their own homes. However, local authority licensing standards and codes may not always permit the offering of nursing supervision within this option. Future demand will nevertheless be for a designed environment that will allow residents to remain in their own dwellings for as long as possible; certainly until at least 24-hour medical/nursing cover is required.

We have to think in terms of making sure that the basic components of independent housing are adaptable if the need arose for residents to receive an increased level of care and support. Of course it will be more costly to develop in the beginning, but you have to frame this against the 60 to 80 year building life. The key to the suitability of future projects will be our understanding and sensitivity to changing needs over time. Buildings that have been designed without the facility for the adequate delivery of services will be very dysfunctional. Dr M. Powell Lawton.

As well as the need to provide an environment that will allow more flexibility in responding to changing functional criteria, consumer demands are pointing to larger space standards. Sheltered housing accommodation began with providing either a bed-sit (efficiency) or one-bedroom apartment. However, as Baker and Parry's research has indicated, two-bedroom units are generally found to sell more quickly than one-bedroom units[1].

When we first started building housing facilities for older people there was a tendency to draw on an institutional experience rather than a hospitality experience. The institutional experience led us to minimise units in relation to housekeeping chores and the maintenance of that unit. However, people will want the kind of space that they have been accustomed to. It's the service and health facilities which are the attraction of these developments, not a minimal size living unit. R. Stephan.

Each generation will expect a little more and certainly the level and allocation of communal health facilities will continue to grow and develop. Each project appears to be taking us a step further away from the images of institution that characterised earlier developments. Russel Greway.

The greatest demand for higher space standards and improved facilities will no doubt come from the private sector. However, it serves as an indication of what even lower income groups would require if they could choose.

We are going to see the more affluent retirees expecting to see the same type of facilities that they have been used to in their own homes. User

In a similar case to that at Wilson Park Philadelphia, two fourteen-storey tower blocks at Birkenhead, UK, which were deemed no longer suitable for family housing by the local council, were converted and totally refurbished to provide sheltered accommodation for older people (photograph: Brock Carmichael Associates).

In a joint venture between public and private sector 206 flats for rent have been provided. Once a blighted and vandalised symbol of urban decay where families queued to move out, the refurbished development has now proved so popular with local elderly people that there is a long waiting list to move in (architects: Brock Carmichael Associates for Wimpey Construction UK Ltd and Wimpey Homes Ltd; photographs: Brock Carmichael Associates).

expectations will rise and certainly the private sector will need to move upscale. Even during the past four years we have noted that the level of demand for more comfort and space is increasing. Andrew Sullivan.

Even in residential homes designed specifically for frail elderly in need of personal or extra care support, the indications are for a move upscale towards the studio apartment with en-suite basic kitchen facilities and bathroom: that is, a move away from the single bed unit.

If a wider range of choice of facilities is offered, site location will increasingly dictate the suitability and marketability of a development.

It is important that people have choices to live in places that are most similar to where they have come from. The closer the two can match, if that is possible, the easier it will be for them to integrate and to continue the socialisation they have known before. Gisela Hill

Therefore, although the concept of retirement homes has traditionally been associated with moving south or to resort areas, this is not necessarily a true reflection of need.

Generally people want to, and should be able, to stay in the locality where they have lived all their lives, so further developments will be determined by the market and economic forces to remain close to existing population centres.
Gilbert Rosenthal

The importance of site location makes it inevitable that greenfield sites will quickly be eaten up and developed. Both private and public developers will invariably turn to re-using existing buildings or upgrading existing housing.

The implications of future trends also point to the necessity to upgrade and bring into line existing facilities for elderly people to cope with future demand.

However, in order to ensure that any errors in facility planning are not merely repeated in future schemes, perhaps we should look to how better to sensitise the designer to the complex and yet often subtle requirements of housing for elderly people.

The process of learning and communication between designer and user group might be further developed to utilise a largely untapped and rich resource of highly practical and relevant design information.

We are still in the early stages of interpreting research and bringing together the design profession, social scientist and gerontologists to communicate and to become sensitized to each others concerns. There is a fundamental necessity for anybody embarking upon a project involving housing for elderly people to spend real time with older people. That is, unobtrusively watching how people use existing environments, as this can often give the designer invaluable clues which may not be available from any other source. I would recommend that the project team should be assembled with a group of, say, ten to fifteen older users, to simply discuss among themselves and with the developers their views on what they feel works and what does not work. I am not convinced that this provides new ideas, but the manner of thinking that older people express has to be valued. Getting the drift of what is important in peoples' lives, even if you may know all the facts, is still a distinct necessity.
Dr M. Powell Lawton.

Finally, the provision of housing, especially for elderly people, cannot be seen in isolation, but rather as one solution in a range of options in the care and support of our elderly population. As previously discussed, there are new and existing developments which will allow elderly people to remain in their own homes. In the United States, senior citizen centers provide day care support in terms of dining and social facilities, particularly in urban areas where new housing programmes may not be possible. In the United Kingdom, local authorities as well as organisations such as Age

Concern and Help the Aged also provide a network of day centres, fulfilling a similar role. Although such centres are currently geared to the less privileged elderly, there is already interest in the private sector in developing day centres on a country club basis, which could be in an existing housing scheme but serve a wide range of the local elderly community.

It must also be emphasised that while the majority of the private development community is heading upmarket, the decrease in directly funded public housing has led demand for other low-cost housing to escalate. The need for public and private sectors to consider how those in lower income groups may still move to more suitable accommodation is perhaps one of the greater challenges for our future.

Another new factor which will also need to be addressed, particularly in the United Kingdom, is the particular need of elderly people from various ethnic groups.

A working party set up by Age Concern and Help the Aged Housing Trust to look into housing for ethnic elders in 1984[2] found that disadvantaged ethnic elderly suffered from the additional problem of not knowing how to obtain advice and help. There was also a lack of awareness amongst service providers, particularly in regard to housing needs.

The implication is that designers must ensure that any special requirements related to religious, dietary or cultural traditional practices are allowed to continue and flourish within the framework of the designed environment. For example, there may be a need for special kitchen facilities, or separate communal facilities for men and women, or for a place of worship. The cooking of certain traditional foods should be discussed to ensure that the right form of cooking appliances are installed, both in the shared kitchens and private dwellings, and that they will be suitable for the preparation of such foods.

Where any such facilities are anticipated there should be close co-operation with representatives from the various community groups concerned, as recommended by the Age Concern/Help the Aged working party.

The field will no doubt continue to diversify and develop. It is hoped, however, that any new directions will increase the choice open to all our elderly and allow them as far as possible the free choice of how to enjoy their retirement years.

It is only fitting that the last word should come from an elderly person who lives in a purpose-built facility:

I came here to be secure, not to have to worry if I fell who would pick me up. I came here because my home was stopping me from doing the things I wanted to do. I came here because here I can be myself. A resident, Golda Meir House, Newton, Mass., USA

References

Introduction

1 Chellis, R.D; Seagle, J.F; Seagle, B.M. *Congregate Housing for Elderly People: a Solution for the 1980s.* Lexington Books, D.C. Heath & Company. Lexington USA 1982.
2 Working Party, *Sheltered Housing for Older People*, Age Concern England, London 1984
3 Baker, S; Parry, M. *Housing for Sale to the Elderly (second report)*, the Housing Research Foundation, London 1984

1 The Building Types Defined

1 Ministry of Housing and Local Government *Housing Standards and Costs: Accommodation specifically designed for Old People.* Circular 82/69, HMSO, London 1969.
2 *Finding Residential & Nursing Home Accommodation*, Age Concern England, Mitcham, Surrey 1986.
3 Butler, A; Oldman, C; Greve, J. *Sheltered Housing for the Elderly*, George Allen and Unwin, London 1983
4 Smith, R.A; Rose, A.M. *An Introduction to the Life Care Industry 1984*, Laventhol and Horwath, Philadelphia 1984

2 Why Such Accommodation is Needed

1 Age Concern England, *Elderly People in the United Kingdom: some Basic Facts*, Age Concern England, Mitcham, Surrey 1985
2 *Social Trends 16* (reproduced with the permission of the Controller of HMSO), HMSO, London 1986
3 Chellis, R.D; Seagle, J.F; Seagle, B.M. *Congregate Housing for Older People: a Solution for the 1980s* (p. 70), Lexington Books, D.C. Heath & Co., Lexington, USA 1982
4 Ibid., p. 1.
5 *Elderly People in the United Kingdom: Some Basic Facts*, Age Concern England, Mitcham, Surrey 1985
6 *Social Trends 16* (reproduced with the permission of the Controller of HMSO), HMSO, London 1986
7 Chellis, R.D; Seagle, J.F; Seagle, B.M. *Congregate Housing for Older People: a Solution for the 1980s* (p. 71), Lexington Books D.C. Heath & Co., Lexington, USA 1982
8 *English House Conditions Survey 1981, part II; Report of the Interview and Local Authority Survey.* (reproduced with the permission of the Controller of HMSO), DOE, London 1983
9 Baker, S; Parry, M. *Housing for Sale to the Elderly, second report*, the Housing Research Foundation, London 1984
10 Baker, S; Parry, M. *Housing for Sale to the Elderly*, the Housing Research Foundation, London 1983
11 Baker, S; Parry, M. *Housing for Sale to the Elderly, third report* (p. 1), the Housing Research Foundation, London 1986
12 Ibid., p. 2.
13 Wheeler, R.S. *Don't Move, We've Got You Covered*, the Institute of Housing, London 1985

3 Who are the Elderly?

1 For details of ergonomic information see Panero, J., Zelnik, M., *Human Dimension and Interior Space*, London, The Architectural Press Ltd, New York, Watson-Guptill Publications 1979

4 An Historical Perspective

1 *The Architects' Journal*, 18 January 1951, The Architectural Press Ltd, London
2 Department of the Environment and Department of Health and Social Security *Housing for Old People*, Joint Discussion Paper 1976
3 Baker, S; Parry, M. *Housing for Sale to the Elderly*, the Housing Research Foundation, London 1983

Further reading
Butler, A; Oldman, C; Greve, J. *Sheltered Housing for the Elderly*, George Allen and Unwin, London 1983
Chellis, R.D; Seagle, J.F; Seagle, B.M. *Congregate Housing for Older People*, D.C. Heath & Co, Lexington, USA 1982

5 Site Selection

1 *Sheltered Housing for Older People* (p. 29) Age Concern England, Mitcham, Surrey 1984

6 Activity-based Design Criteria

1 Scottish Housing Handbook, *Housing for the Elderly*, (reproduced with the permission of the Controller of HMSO), HMSO, Edinburgh and London 1980
2 Howell, S.C. *Designing for Aging: Patterns of Use*, MIT Press, Cambridge, Mass. 1980
3 Ibid.
4 Ibid.
5 Salmon, G. *Abbeyfield Extra Care Manual* (p. 71), The Abbeyfield Society, St Albans, Herts 1982
6 Butler, A; Oldman, C; Greve, J. *Sheltered Housing for the Elderly*, George Allen & Unwin, London 1983
7 Salmon, G. *Abbeyfield Extra Care Manual*, the Abbeyfield Society, Herts 1982
8 Ibid.
9 Ibid.
10 Scottish Housing Handbook, *Housing for the Elderly*, (reproduced with the permission of the Controller of HMSO), Scottish Development Department/HMSO, Edinburgh 1980
11 Wilshere, E.R. *Equipment for the Disabled: Housing and Furniture* (pp. 33–4), 5th edition. Oxfordshire Health Authority, Nuffield Orthopaedic Centre, Oxford 1986
12 Howell, S.C. *Designing for Aging: Patterns for Use* (p. 129), MIT Press, Cambridge, Mass. 1980
13 Ibid.
14 *Sheltered Housing for Older People* (p. 15), Age Concern England, Mitcham, Surrey 1984
15 Howell, S.C. *Designing for Aging: Patterns for Use* (pp. 133–212), MIT Press, Cambridge, Mass. 1980
16 Howell, S.C. *Congregate Housing. Design, Evaluation Project*, MIT Department of Architecture, Cambridge, Mass. 1977
17 Baker, S; Parry, M. *Housing for Sale to the Elderly, third report* (p. 12), the Housing Research Foundation, London 1986
18 Howell, S.C. *Storage: Putting Things Away. Design Evaluation Project* (p. 12), MIT Department of Architecture, Cambridge, Mass. 1979
For further information on the design and layout of kitchens and bathrooms see *Sheltered Housing for the Elderly*, Tectonics, London, 1984
19 For information about training and job descriptions of wardens see *Sheltered Housing for Older People* (pp. 53–89), Age Concern England, Mitcham, Surrey 1984
20 Baker, S; Parry, M. *Housing for Sale to the Elderly, third report* (p. 36), the Housing Research Foundation, London 1986
21 Housing Design Brief: *Housing for Elderly People*, the Institute of Housing/Royal Institute of British Architects, Section LO3, London 1986

7 Environmental Hardware and Services

1 For detailed evaluation of design of windows see Howell, S.C; Epp, G. *Windows: Design Evaluation Project*, MIT Department of Architecture, Cambridge, Mass. 1976

Further reading
Templeton, D; Saunders, D. *Acoustic Design.* the Architectural Press Ltd., London 1987
Butler, A. 'Dispersed Alarm Systems for the Elderly' (pp. 17–23), *Social Work Service No. 25*, January 1981
Baker, S; Parry, M. 'Review of Dispersed Alarm Systems' (pp. 24–28), *Housing 20/9*, 1984
'Alarm systems in elderly persons housing' (pp. 318–321), *Which?* magazine, July 1986

8 New Directions

1 Baker, S; Parry, M. *Housing for Sale to the Elderly, third report*, the Housing Research Foundation, London 1986
2 *Housing for Ethnic Elders* (report of working party set up by Age Concern and Help the Aged Housing Trust) Age Concern England/Help the Aged Housing Trust, Mitcham, Surrey, 1984

10

Bibliography

This bibliography cites a selection of the more recent books and articles related to the design of housing for elderly people.

Age Concern/National Housing and Town Planning Council, *A Buyer's Guide to Sheltered Housing*, London 1985.

Age Concern/Help the Aged Housing Trust, *Housing for Ethnic Elders*, Mitcham, Surrey, UK 1984.

Age Concern England, *Housing for Older People*, Mitcham, Surrey, UK 1984.

Baker, S.; Parry, M. *Housing for Sale to the Elderly*, The Housing Research Foundation, London 1983.

Baker, S.; Parry, M. *Housing for Sale to the Elderly, second report*, The Housing Research Foundation, London 1984.

Baker, S.; Parry, M. *Housing for Sale to the Elderly, third report*, The Housing Research Foundation, London 1986.

Breger, W. H.; Pomeranz, W. R. *Nursing Home Development*, Van Nostrand Reinhold, New York 1985.

Butler, A.; Oldman, C.; Greve, J. *Sheltered Housing for the Elderly*, George Allen & Unwin, London 1983.

Cambridge Geriatric Liaison Committee, *The Design of Sheltered Housing*, Cambridge, UK 1975.

Carstens, D. Y. *Site Planning and Design for the Elderly*, Van Nostrand Reinhold, New York 1985.

Chellis, R. D.; Seagle, J. F.; Seagle, B. M. *Congregate Housing for Older People*, Lexington Books, D. C. Heath, Lexington, Mass. USA 1982.

City of Wakefield Municipal District Council, *Housing and Elderly People*, Wakefield UK 1985.

Davies, R. H. *Housing for the Elderly*, Ethel Percy Andrus Gerontology Center, University of Southern California, Los Angeles 1973.

Goldenberg, L. *Housing for the Elderly: New Trends in Europe*, Garland STPM Press, New York 1981.

Goldsmith, S. *Designing for the Disabled*, third edition, RIBA Publications Ltd, London 1976.

Green, I.; Fedewa, B. E.; Johnston, C. A.; Jackson, W. M.; Deardorff, H. C. *Housing for the Elderly: the Development and Design Process*, Van Nostrand Reinhold, New York 1975.

Her Majesty's Stationery Office, *Managing Social Services for the Elderly More Effectively*, HMSO, London 1985.

Hoglunid, J. D. *Housing for the Elderly: Privacy and Independence in Environments for Aging*, Van Nostrand Reinhold, New York 1985.

Howell, S. C. *Design for Aging: Patterns of Use*, MIT Press, Cambridge, Mass. 1980.

Hunt, J. *Housing and Care for Elderly People*, Cwmbran Development Corporation and Torfaen Borough Council, Cwmbran, Wales 1985.

House Builder's Federation/National Housing and Town Planning Council, *Sheltered Housing for Sale*, London 1985.

Institute of Housing/Royal Institute of British Architects, *Housing Design Brief: Housing for Elderly People*, London 1986.

Lawton, M. P. *Changing Service Needs of Older Tenants: Proposals to the Administration of Aging*, Philadelphia Geriatric Center, Philadelphia 1979.

National Federation of Housing Associations, *Leasehold Sheltered Housing*, London 1985.

Newcomer, R. J.; Lawton, M. P.; Byerts, T. O. *Housing an Aging Society: Issues, Alternatives and Policy*, Van Nostrand Reinhold, New York 1986.

Norman, A. *Bricks and Mortals: Design and Lifestyle in Old Peoples' Homes*, Centre for Policy on Ageing, London 1984.

Nouwen, H. J. M.; Gaffney, W. J. *Aging: the Fulfilment of Life*, Image Books, New York 1986.

Penton, J. H. *Providing for Disabled Visitors*, English Tourist Board/Holiday Care Service, London 1985.

Progressive Architecture, 'The Age of Aging', *PA* August 1981, pp. 59–75.

Raschko, B. B. *Housing Interiors for the Disabled and Elderly*, Van Nostrand Reinhold, New York 1982.

Regnier, V. *Planning for the Elderly*, Ethel Percy Andrus Gerontology Center, University of Southern California, Los Angeles 1979.

Rose, E. A. *Housing for the Aged*, Teakfield Ltd/Jurue, Birmingham, UK 1978.

Rose, E. A. *Housing Needs and the Elderly*, Gower Publishing, Aldershot, UK 1982.

Salmon, G. *Abbeyfield Extra-care Manual*, The Abbeyfield Society, St Albans, UK 1982.

Saxby, J. H. *Dwellings for the Elderly*, Housing Corporation of New Zealand, NZ 1980.

Scottish Development Department, *Scottish Housing Handbook: Housing for the Elderly*, HMSO, Edinburgh and London 1980.

Steinfield, E. *Barrier-Free Design for the Elderly and the Disabled*, Syracuse University Gerontology Center and Center for Instructional Development, New York 1975.

Tectonics, *Sheltered Housing for the Elderly: Design Criteria*, Tectonics, London 1984.

Thorpe, S. *Designing for People with Sensory Impairments*, Centre on Environment for the Handicapped, London 1986.

Thorpe, S. *Housing Design Sheets*, Centre on Environment for the Handicapped, London 1985.

Tinker, A. *The Elderly in Modern Society*, second edition, Longman, London 1984.

Townsend, P. *The Last Refuge*, Routledge and Kegan Paul, London 1962.

Urban Land Institute, *Housing for a Maturing Population*, Urban Land Institute, Washington, USA 1983.

Valins, M. 'Options in Retirement Housing', *Design for Special Needs No. 38*, September/December 1985, Centre on Environment for the Handicapped, London.

Valins, M. 'The American Experience', *Retirement Homes* June/July 1987, issue no. 7. The Sellwood Press Ltd.

Zeisel, J.; Epp, G.; Demos, S. *Low Rise Housing for Older People: Behavioral Criteria for Design*, Washington U.S. Department of Housing & Urban Development Office of Policy Development and Research, Washington, USA 1977.

11

Index